CHINA IMAGINED

GREGORY B. LEE

China Imagined

From European Fantasy to Spectacular Power

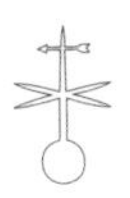

HURST & COMPANY, LONDON

First published in the United Kingdom in 2018 by
C. Hurst & Co. (Publishers) Ltd.,
41 Great Russell Street, London, WC1B 3PL

Distributed in the United States, Canada and Latin America by
Oxford University Press, 198 Madison Avenue, New York, NY 10016,
United States of America.

A Cataloguing-in-Publication data record for this book
is available from the British Library.

ISBN: 9781787380165

This book is printed using paper from registered sustainable
and managed sources.

www.hurstpublishers.com

Printed in Great Britain by Bell & Bain Ltd, Glasgow

CONTENTS

CONTENTS

LIST OF ILLUSTRATIONS

MAPS

MAPS

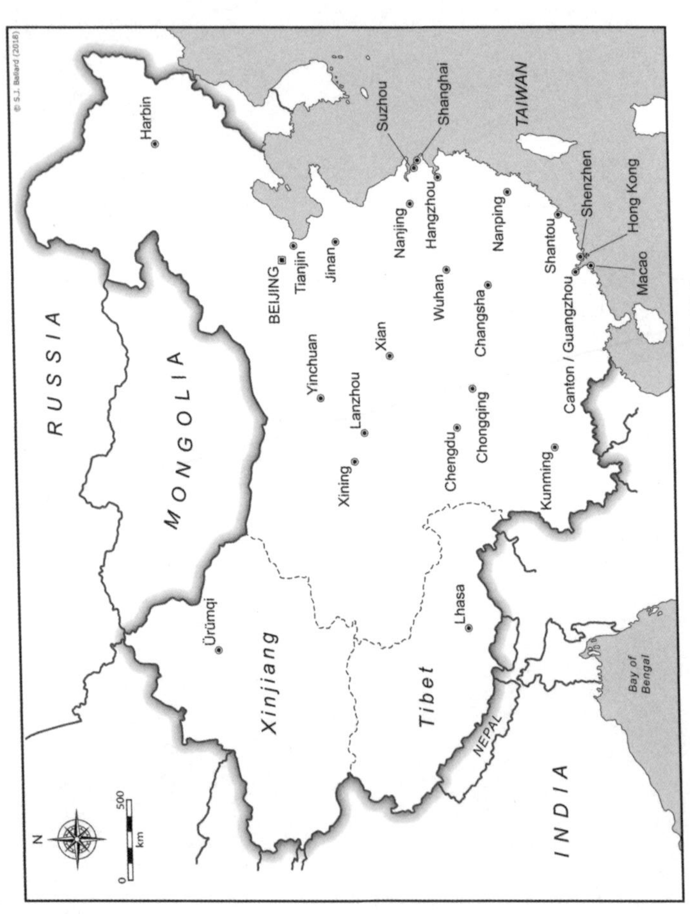

Map1: The People's Republic of China

MAPS

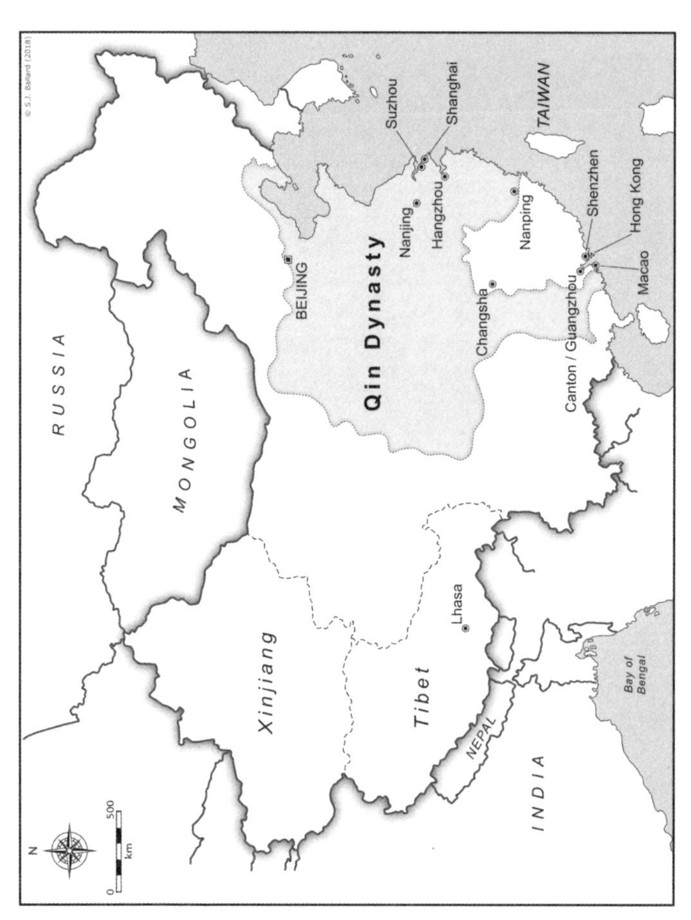

Map 2: China-Before-China—Qin Dynasty territory (3rd century BCE)

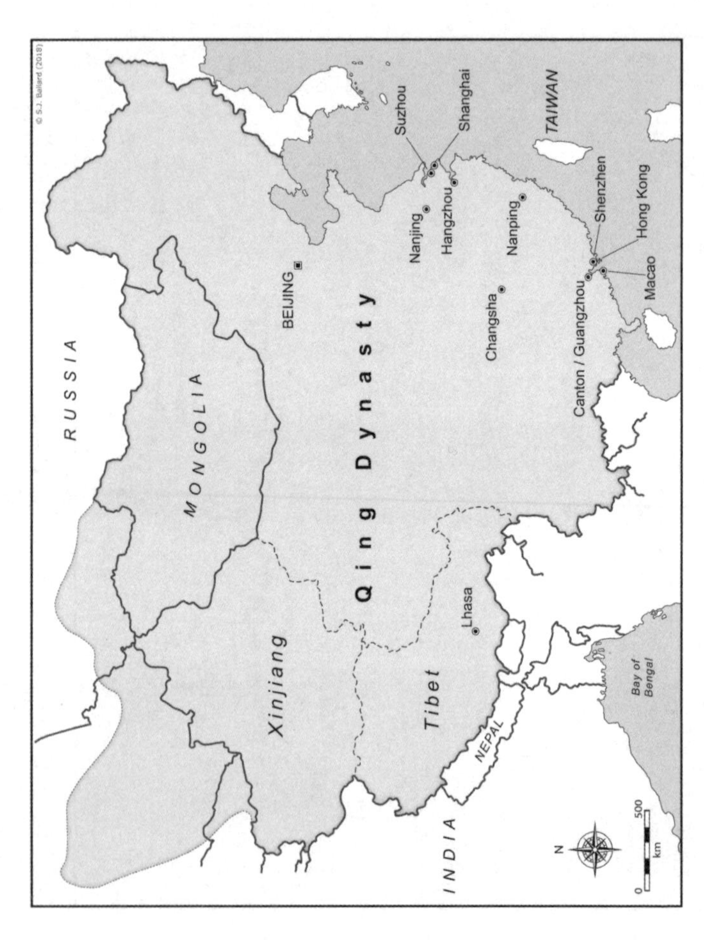

Map 3: China-Before-China—extent of Qing Dynasty (1644–1912) in 1850

CHRONOLOGY

c. 7000–2000 BCE	Neolithic period
c. 2800–2100 BCE	Age of Five Rulers (mythical)
c. 2100–256 BCE	Bronze Age
	c. 2100–1600 BCE Xia dynasty
	c. 1600–1050 BCE Shang dynasty
	c. 1046–256 BCE Zhou dynasty
221–206 BCE	Qin dynasty (unification)
	Standardized literary language, wenyan 文言, *used as state and elite written language from this period until 20th century.*
206 BCE–206 CE	Han dynasty (consolidation of unified territories)
220–265 CE	Three Kingdoms period
265–420	Jin dynasty (Sima/Liang Jin)
420–589	Northern and Southern dynasties period
	317–86 Southern dynasties
	386–581 Northern dynasties
590–618	Sui dynasty
618–906	Tang dynasty
907–960	Five Dynasties period
960–1279	Song dynasty
	1115–1234 Jin dynasty (Great Jin)
1271–1368	Yuan dynasty (Mongols)

CHRONOLOGY

1368–1644	Ming dynasty *Officials start using Nanjing Mandarin, or* guanhua 官話, *as spoken standard. Vernacular language,* baihua 白話, *used for 'non-serious' fiction.* *From 16th c.: Europeans begin using the term 'China'.*
1644–1912	Qing dynasty (Manchus) *Mid-19th c.: reformers start using 'China'* (Zhongguo 中國) *to refer to the country as a nation-state.* *Late 19th c.: reformers adopt Mandarin as spoken norm.* *Early 20th c.:* Guoyu 國語, *based on Mandarin, established as the national language.*
1912–1949	Republic of China *1920s: Wenyan largely displaced as common written language. Writers use the modernized vernacular* (baihua) *to create a national literature and language.*
1949–	People's Republic of China Putonghua 普通話, *the 'common language' based on* guoyu, *adopted as the national language.*

CHINAS IMAGINED

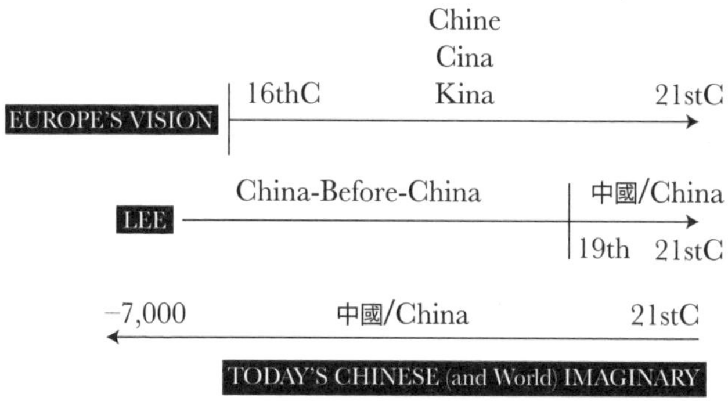

Chine
Cina
Kina

EUROPE'S VISION | 16thC → 21stC

LEE | China-Before-China → 中國/China (19th – 21stC)

–7,000 ← 中國/China ← 21stC

TODAY'S CHINESE (and World) IMAGINARY

PREFATORY NOTE

This book addresses and attempts to answer some seemingly straightforward questions about China: what is it? Where has it come from? Where is it going? These are things I have been asking myself since I was a child. For, although my involvement with the formal, academic study of China began only some four decades ago, my hearing about China and my acquaintance with Chinese people stretches back to my childhood and to my grandfather. Chan Chun Lee left what was not yet China, but rather the land ruled over by the Manchu dynasty, shortly before its fall, in 1911.

From my birth until my grandfather's death some seven years later, I spent much of my young everyday life by his side. I lived in his house, listening to him talk to compatriots as I played on the living-room floor, watching him make noodles starting with just flour and water, and accompanying him on outings to Chinatown and its outposts. Then one day he was no more, and I missed him and the life I had shared with him. It was that loss, that lack, that eventually led me to want to learn Chinese, to go and see China for myself; a China he had imagined throughout his lifetime, and to which he had always planned to return.[1]

By the time my grandfather arrived in Europe, the collapsing Manchu order—which had expanded and ruled over the territory Europeans by then sometimes called China, sometimes Tartary, sometimes the Celestial Empire—had been overthrown. When he left Canton in the summer of 1911, the Republic of China did not exist. For the remainder of his life, a life he would spend in Britain, he would observe the process of the creation of China the nation-state, from a distance. In a sense he incarnated the new Chinese citizen. He had a vision of China as a modern country, he saw himself as part of it, and even with my child's eyes I could see that he was proud of who he was. Dressed in his dark suit and starched, stiff shirt collars, he had adopted modern—that is to say Western—dress, not so as to become a Westerner, but in order to be Chinese; that is, to belong to and to represent China the nation-state. Please bear him in mind as you read what follows.

ACKNOWLEDGMENTS

I should like first to thank my family for their patience and encouragement; they are always the ones to bear the brunt when a writing project is under way. My gratitude goes to Isabelle for her always sensible advice and her re-reading, to Vanessa for her re-reading and academic companionship, and not least to Natacha who imagined and executed the illustration on which the cover design of this book is based.

My thanks go also to Vanessa Frangville whose invitation to present a keynote address at a conference at the Université libre de Bruxelles obliged me to crystallize thoughts that had been in gestation for some years; that lecture constituted the starting point of this book.

My friends and colleagues in postcolonial studies Iain Chambers and Johan Höglund read an early draft and provided encouraging comments, and my conversations with Sanjay Seth and Francisco Carballo on modernity and the nation-state were also invaluable. Lidia Curti's rich and extensive intellectual culture also inspired me, while closer to home both Florent Villard and Sophie Coavoux, who could write a similar book about Greece, have listened to me talk on the ideas contained in this book over a number of years. Neither must I forget Alex Hamilton who kindly acted as 'general reader' for an early draft. Likewise, my long-suffering students at the University of Lyon, in particular those attending my Master's and Doctoral seminars, provided me with a regular conversation on the questions addressed here as the manuscript progressed. Old friends and colleagues Craig Clunas and Michael Dutton have provided inspiration through their own intellectual projects and the thoughts we have shared together. I should also like to express my gratitude to Jean-Patrice Boudet for conversations on 'France before France' and the belated emergence of a French national consciousness. Conversations held over the past few decades with friends and scholars Harry Harootunian, Jean François Billeter, Anne Cheng and Philippe Pelletier have also resonated in my mind as I wrote this book; they have all shed light on the historical realities that constitute China and Japan. Naturally, none of those mentioned above are to be held responsible for anything objectionable that the reader may find in these pages.

I should like to thank both Professor Isabel Morais who invited me to talk about the book in Macau, and Chinese colleagues and students who welcomed both me and my thoughts on China in Guangdong in the late spring of 2018. The feedback I received from both audiences was heartwarming and reassuring.

I must thank my publisher Michael Dwyer for not shying away from what I presented to him a year ago as a potentially controversial book. My gratitude goes also to the rest of the Hurst team and in particular to my editor Lara Weisweiller-Wu, for her extremely attentive re-reading of the manuscript and her sensible and empathetic suggestions, and to Daisy Leitch. My thanks also to my proof-reader, Erin, for doing such a meticulous job.

Lastly, I am indebted to many more scholars than I have cited in the notes and the bibliography, but I should like to pay homage in particular to two great twentieth-century thinkers who are often neglected by the academic world: Jacques Ellul, a visionary intellectual who rang the alarm bells concerning the environmental nightmare in which we now find ourselves, and Cornelius Castoriadis, whose exemplary intellectual honesty and grasp of what real democracy could be remain unparalleled.

PART ONE

FROM CHINA-BEFORE-CHINA TO CHINA THE NATION

INTRODUCTION

"Who controls the past controls the future. Who controls the present controls the past."

George Orwell, *1984*

For several centuries now, European and American sinologists and novelists have imagined their own China, and have narrated and imposed China according to this imaginary. By imaginary, I mean that clutch of phrases, images and beliefs which make up the commonly held understanding we have of a group or community (be it an ethnicity or a nation, our own or someone else's), and which dictates the way we perceive it or them.

Thus far, this Western imaginary of China has been globally dominant. But now, in the twenty-first century, 'China', whose shape and form and categories we in the West invented and maintained, is starting to escape us. The 'China' we have created, that we have imagined, that we have dreamt up and of which we have dreamt—the China that frightened us as well as fascinated us—has slipped our grasp. We no longer have sole control over it; just as the West's dominance over the world's economy has waned, so has its ability to impose the planet's global story. But before attempting to take stock of today's China, we need to understand where that China has come from.

We all know where China is, even if its present and its desired boundaries are contested by both China itself and its neighbours. But how far does this 'entity' called 'China' stretch back? To the early traces of 'civilization' in the space now occupied by China, thus between four and seven millennia or more? To the unification under the short-lived Qin[i] dynasty in 221 BCE? To the European use of the name 'China' in the sixteenth century? Or to the establishment of the 'Republic of China' in 1912, when the 'Chinese' administration first employed the term?[1]

For, however far back we may trace the elite cultural practices and succession of ruling dynasties that have occupied the space that is now called 'China', what is undeniable is that the popular collective consciousness of a nation called 'China', or *Zhongguo* 中國,[ii] is very recent indeed. As to what is, and what in the past has constituted, China—in terms of ethnicity, geography, language, culture, religion and politics—the question is both vast and complex. This book attempts to go beyond the glib or conventional responses to the question: 'What and when is China?'

To begin with, where does the word 'China' come from? Not from the land we now call China, that much is certain. In the early sixteenth century, in 1516, a certain Portuguese travel writer named Duarte Barbosa employed the term. Later it occurs in several European languages: as *Cina* in Italy, as *Chine* in France, and in English as China. The Spaniards, arriving from Mexico in the mid-sixteenth century, rapidly colonized what would become the Philippines, and from there ventured into what was still Ming dynasty territory that they would call China. They thus participated significantly in the propagation of the word and the imaginary of 'China'. One such adventurer was the soldier Miguel de Loarca, who in 1575 accompanied Father Martín de Rada on a diplomatic

i. Pronounced as in the English *chin*.

ii. *Zhongguo*: *zhong* pronounced like 'jung' as in Northern English 'jungle', and *guo* to rhyme with 'war' or 'law'.

mission to China, setting out from the Philippines, which would become increasingly important as a site of stories and information with which the Spanish built up their imagined China. Loarca is responsible for one of the first Western works on 'China'.[2] Commenting on this and other early Spanish writings, Beatriz Moncó tells us that 'the image of China was created gradually, through snippets of memory, through personal experiences, which gave rise to specific visions of that which was China'.[3] Here, Moncó is describing the accumulation of minor writings that nevertheless were fundamental to an imagined 'China' that was entirely European.

In what we now call South-East Asia, it seems that a variant of 'China' was used to designate a neighbour to the north, and as the sinologist Jeff Wade has demonstrated, *Zina* designated a state in the south of what is now known as China, a territory inhabited by the Lolo and Yi peoples, and thus not by those who would become known as the Han, or by Westerners as simply 'the Chinese'.[4] In what the Europeans would call China, no polity or society ever used the name 'China or any variants of such'.[5]

For several centuries, then, Europeans employed the word China to describe, narrate, and map the territory governed by the Ming rulers and later by the Manchus. After the fall of the Ming dynasty and the installation of the Qing[iii] by the Manchu people in 1644, the term 'Tartary' was also employed, as was 'the Celestial Empire'. But neither the Manchu rulers nor the ruled had use for this foreign word 'China'. Moreover, an equivalent for it was not sought, needed or employed until the nineteenth century, with its foreign power treaties and emerging ideologies of a nation-state; until then the people, or rather peoples, we called 'Chinese' simply had no need for it.

iii. Pronounced 'ching' as in Chingford.

As the Qing dynasty progressed, European admiration and fascination turned to brutality and aggression. A new denigratory way of framing 'China' was necessary to justify Western encroachment and it was to be found in the mid-nineteenth century theories of scientific racism. The subjects of the Qing dynasty and later the citizens of the 1912 Republic needed to be portrayed as inferiors, decadent, incapable of modern thought, in short unfit to run a modern state. In particular, it had to be shown that the Chinese mind was inadequate. From the end of the nineteenth century to the middle of the twentieth, both serious and popular writers on China relied on a set of stereotypes first popularized by an American missionary, Arthur Smith. In his 1890 work *Chinese Characteristics* he described what he saw as the deficiencies of the Chinese mind thus:

> He does not understand, because he does not expect to understand, and it takes him an appreciable time to get such intellectual forces as he has, into a position to be used at all. His mind is like a rusty old smooth-bore cannon mounted on an old decrepit carriage … Another mark of intellectual torpor is the inability of an ordinary mind to entertain an idea, and then pass it on to another in its original shape.[6]

Everything good about China was projected onto its past, its now decadent, decrepit and sickly population deemed unsuited to the challenges of modernity. Thus, over forty years after Smith's book was published, a French China specialist with numerous China books to his name, Jean Rodes, could write at the beginning of the 1930s:

> The power of control over the brain being less developed in the Chinese, he, under certain conditions of agitation, is overtaken by all sorts of subconscious and uncontrolled reflexes, dorsal column automatism … [in which can be seen] an irremediable

cause of racial inferiority, which had so enchanted Count Gobineau.[7]

Gobineau was a famous, now notorious, mid-nineteenth-century theorist of scientific racism, whose theories on the Aryan master race helped legitimize and justify nineteenth-century colonialist expansion in Africa and Asia. His work influenced the anti-Semitic stance adopted by Richard Wagner, and was later, in a redacted form, required reading for the German Nazi leadership. Convinced, as was Wagner, that China would invade Europe, he was also instrumental in spreading fear of the 'Yellow Peril' amongst the German aristocracy and beyond.

Western racist literary and journalistic representations thus straddled the end of the Qing and the early decades of the Republic of China. For the purveyor of racist stereotypes, nothing had changed; it was after all the West that had invented 'China', 'Chinese' and, of course, 'the Chinaman'.[8] With the legitimation of scientific racism, Europe—soon to be followed by Japan and the United States—had entered a new phase of colonialism marked by imperialist expansion, driven by industrial capitalist needs for resources and markets. The nineteenth century, then, saw confrontation between imperialist powers, particularly Britain, on the one hand and the Qing dynasty on the other. The Manchu bureaucratic elite found itself obliged to take account of this Western imaginary, which located and described them all as 'Chinese' and called the territory they inhabited 'China'.

As for the Manchus' urban-dwelling subjects, it was primarily their distaste for this foreign ruling house that fuelled the rise of a state-wide identity; I stipulate 'urban-dwelling' since the vast majority of China's population, something like 90 per cent in the nineteenth century, was made up of illiterate peasants, largely ignorant of belonging to any sort of nation or political entity. In addition, the Manchus went out of their way to flaunt and bolster their ethnic difference, doing so by showing themselves as standing out against the majority Han population. While the Manchus ruled over and even extended the boundaries of what the West was already calling China, they took care to maintain a hallowed ancestral land that would be called Manchuria, a process embedded in the rulers' ambition 'to emphasize the distinctiveness of the Manchu people vis-a-vis the Han Chinese as well as with their desire clearly to demarcate the extent of the territory under Qing control.'[9] Thus the existence of a Han identity was in part due to the Manchus' emphasizing their own exclusive difference.

So much for the role of the Manchus in the emergence of a Han national consciousness. As for the West's experts and specialists, they had long been treating this vast and ethnically, culturally and linguistically complex land as a homogeneous entity. And thus the elision of China the nation-state with what came before, what Western sinologists would call 'imperial China' and/or 'ancient China', has historically been a largely unproblematic one for such specialists. For Westerners, 'China', until mid-way through the twentieth century, was synonymous with a 'civilization' that had existed, indeed flourished, for several thousands of years, in the space Europe had called 'China' since the sixteenth century. The question of contemporary China was, for pre-Cold War sinologists, inexistent, except insofar as physical traces and vestiges of 'civilization' could be found on China's territory.

For instance, take the renowned, erudite scientist and sinologist Joseph Needham, whose influential, monumental work *Science and Civilisation in China* addressed the evolution of a specifically 'Chinese' technology over the period of time corresponding to dynastic history.[10] The first volume of this study appeared in 1954. For Needham, the ruling dynasties were already 'Chinese' dynasties, and the ruled already 'Chinese' ('it may be mentioned that the Chinese counted [years], as in medieval Europe, from the accession of their kings or emperors').[11] Needham seems to understand 'the Chinese', both rulers and the ruled, in racial, or ethnic terms; presumably as Han. We learn that it is 'unfortunate that the only exhaustive analysis of a single Chinese dynasty ... in a Western language, concerns a dynasty which was not really Chinese at all—the Liao.[iv] We refer to the monumental book of Wittfogel, Fêng Chia-shêng *et al*'.[12] Thus, if the rulers were not 'ethnically' Chinese, as we might say today, the dynasty was 'not really Chinese at all', and China/Chinese is being understood ethnically and not territorially here. Without ever having defined, in the first seventy pages of his work, precisely who 'the Chinese' were, Needham simply invokes a shared author/reader imaginary of a racially and historically homogeneous and identifiable people, culture and language.

It is not only Western sinologists who bemoan the passing of an 'authentic' China. There is also a modern-day Chinese view that holds that, in seeking to become strong and sovereign, China, by dint of imitating the West, has lost its Chineseness; and that in following the economic, political and technological logic of the modern world and its epistemologies, China has quite simply become the West.[v]

iv. Liao 了 was a dynasty which for two centuries (907–1125 CE) controlled a large part of what is now northern China.

v. This is a contradiction that will be addressed at length later in this book. For now, let me simply remind the reader of the Chinese Communist Party's 2017 campaign to discourage the celebration of Christmas, despite having used the same festival in the past as an excuse for excessive consumption—Christmas falling a few weeks before Chinese New Year, it provides a perfect opportunity for a prolonged period of consumerist bingeing. See Clover, 'China accused of waging war on Christmas': 'Throughout China, local governments, Communist party branches,

But this analysis needs to be tempered, nuanced and reconsidered. For if we accept 'China' as a concept, an entity invented in the West and subsequently naturalized, internalized and translated as *Zhongguo* 中國 (the central country) at the end of the Manchus' reign, and if we accept the modernity of this nation-state, which for most of the twentieth century was a nation-state in the making, then we can perceive China quite differently. We can understand that the establishment of this nation-state in the space that we now call China never was, except for a sprinkling of idealists, a project of Renaissance, of rebirth, of rising from the ashes of an eternal China. In fact, if 'China' was a project of nation-making, there cannot have been any loss of identity, except the loss of non-national local cultures, languages and customs.[vi] On the contrary, China can be seen as having been created, its national identity forged, during the twentieth century. For the first time in human history, a really existing polity called China was crafted and made. China did not lose its identity; it gained one. China was created.[vii]

Indeed, the project underlying the establishment of this nation-state was precisely the creation of something else. Even

---

schools and even shopping malls issued regulations this year suggesting people tone down Christmas parties and decorations. The government insists there is no actual ban of Christmas in place at the national level but the number of local bans have raised questions about whether there is a behind-the-scenes "war on Christmas" by Beijing.'

vi. In the process of creating the nation-state, local customs or cultural and linguistic practices are weakened or destroyed; some will form the basis, as has been the case in China, for the creation of national-level practices. It is the loss of these community-level practices that leads to the nostalgia and new mythology inspiring separatist dreams of yet newer nations, as though the dead-end nineteenth-century paradigm of nationalism could provide the solutions demanded by the excesses and the heteronomy of the twenty-first.

vii. Here again the word 'create' is used advisedly.

for those seeking a 'rebirth' of a mythic lost glory—in a backward-looking imaginary that venerated the past as a halcyon epoch to be regained, much as Confucius had looked back to past dynastic glories in the fourth century BCE—their project first necessitated the creation of this 'something else'.[viii] During the twentieth century, we witnessed various expressions of this 'something else'. Today we see a China that has reached a stage of existence that corresponds to the ambition, or vision, of those who dreamt it. Premodern 'China', what I call in this book China-Before-China, is now simply part of the imaginary of today's really existing China.

viii. Confucius, in his political philosophy, sought the unification of 'the central states' by privileging the past.

1

WHAT AND WHEN IS CHINA?

So when and what is China? If we attempt to unpack the proper nouns and adjectives used in Chinese to define and describe the country, people and language that in English we call China and Chinese, we then understand immediately the inadequacy of these two English words. If we compare everything that is hidden behind the terms 'China' and 'Chinese' in English with the words employed in what we now call modern standard Chinese (or 'Mandarin') to name this entity, this 'people' who are not, by any definition, one people—to describe this language which seems monolithic and yet is multiple—we start to grasp their complexity. Below is a list, not an exhaustive one, of terms in Chinese which contain within them a number of meanings and nuances, but which are often, innocently or otherwise, simply translated into English as 'China' or 'Chinese'—by the Chinese authorities and their English-language media, by sinologists and China experts. Each of these terms, both proper nouns and adjectives, needs to be unpacked, historicized, contextualized. This may seem a forbidding exercise, but bear with it and you will see the extent of the problem of this under-translation, of both the Chinese reality today and what preceded it.

Let us take first the proper noun adjective *Zhongguo* 中國, which translates the polity and/or territory, China. The range of meanings it has to cover is vast. It can refer simply to China, today's modern nation-state, which officially is called the People's Republic of China or PRC. It may also signify the Chinese government or authorities, as in 'China's policy on pollution', when we mean the Chinese government's policy. 'China' is also used transhistorically, or ahistorically, to mean not only China the modern nation-state, but also the state during the dynastic periods, and the prehistoric civilizations found within the space now occupied by the PRC. The word *zhongguo* can also translate as the 'central states' or 'central kingdoms' that existed before their unification—or rather absorption—by the Qin state and what became the short-lived Qin dynasty (221–206 BCE). The unified state was consolidated by the Han dynasties ('Western Han' 206 BCE–9 CE; 'Eastern Han' 25–220 CE), which would give rise to the denomination 'Han' to describe the subjects of China's dynasties thereafter; however, the connotation that links 'Han' to an ethnicity is a modern one. Geographically, *Da Zhongguo*, literally 'Big China' but usually translated 'Greater China', refers to China as a spatially larger unit which includes mainland China, Hong Kong, Macao, and Taiwan.

The proper noun and adjective *Zhonghua* 中華 (China/Chinese) also denotes the territory and polity that is China. However, *Zhonghua* is a higher register of language than *Zhongguo* and is used in the official names of both modern republics: *Zhonghua minguo* 中華民國 for the Republic of China (1912–49); and *Zhonghua renmin gongheguo* 中華人民共和國 for the People's Republic of China (1949–). The former is still the official name for the state known as Taiwan, where the nationalist government sought refuge when it fled the mainland in 1949. The proper noun *Da Zhonghua* 大中華 translates as 'Greater China' and again is used more broadly to designate mainland China, Taiwan, Hong Kong, Macao, and even the Chinese Diaspora.

Zhongguoren 中國人 may refer to a Chinese (person) or the Chinese (people). The word became known in Britain to a whole generation of Monty Python fans when the popular comedians recorded the 1980 song 'I Like Chinese', which included a verse sung in Chinese: '*Wo ai Zhongguoren*', literally 'I like Chinese'.[i] *Zhongguoren* may more specifically refer to a citizen of the PRC, and thus include Tibetans and Uighurs.

The word *Huaren* 華人 is an inclusive term meaning 'a Chinese person' or 'Chinese people' and may refer to all those in China proper while also denoting those outside China proper in the diaspora. The term *Huaqiao* is usually translated as 'Overseas Chinese' and more specifically refers to Chinese living abroad or descendants of those who have emigrated.

As for the term *Han* 漢, it is assumed by scholars trained in the dominant tradition of sinology that 'Han' is generally equal to 'Chinese'—a convention maintained by the current regime. Han is used in China today to refer to what the authorities have defined as the main ethnic group in China. However, originally it referred to those seeing themselves as descending from the first relatively long dynastic period, the Han, which consolidated the process of unification and homogenization started by the short-lived Qin. There originally was no connotation of race or ethnicity. Nowadays, the term *Hanren* 漢人, literally 'Han person' or 'Han people', which again we generally translate outside China as 'Chinese', refers to a member of

i. The song is to be found on the album *Contractual Obligation* released on the Charisma (UK) and Arista (US) labels in October 1980. It was also issued as a single in the UK in the same month, and again in 1989, with the Chinese characters for 'I like Chinese' (我愛中國人) featuring on the sleeves. The song's lyrics were infused with orientalist and racist stereotypes redolent of George Formby's 1930s lyrics recounting the adventures of Mr Wu the Laundryman. When the Pythons were reconstituted for a 2014 concert, some of the offending lyrics were replaced.

the Han majority ethnicity (91 per cent of China's current population as officially defined by the PRC state). This group is, nevertheless, 'comprised of a wide variety of culturally and ethnically diverse populations, including eight mutually unintelligible linguistic groupings (Mandarin, Wu, Yue, Xiang, Hakka, Gan, Southern and Northern Min).'[1]

Similarly, 唐人 *Tangren* is a term used by those who see their 'Chineseness' as stemming from a later period, the Tang dynasty (618–907 CE), when the southern parts of what is now China and their populations were absorbed into the dynastic territories of the Tang. The term *Tangren* is used primarily by Cantonese-speaking southerners, especially in Hong Kong, and by those in the diaspora who emigrated in the nineteenth century from the south. Thus what is called 'Chinatown' in English was called *Tangrenjie* 唐人街 in Chinese, which translates literally as 'Tang-Person Street'. The word for Chinatown used by the Chinese authorities, *Zhongguocheng* 中國城, now found inscribed on the world's Chinatown arches—which are often paid for by Chinese municipalities—is a late twentieth-century neologism and is no more than a back-translation of the English 'Chinatown'.[ii] Again a wealth of complex history is erased in the translation of *Tangren* by 'Chinese', an erasure the authorities have been happy to embrace.

Then come the terms we use to describe the language(s) spoken in China today and in the past. In English we refer indiscriminately to 'Chinese'. In China itself we find *Zhongwen* 中文, which we could translate literally as 'China writing'. The word carries no connotation of the historical moment

ii. For instance, the Liverpool arch constructed in 1999–2000 was financed by Liverpool's sister city Shanghai and built by engineers and artisans from China. It was squeezed into the narrow confines of Nelson Street, the post-World War II Chinatown, where it towers over nothing in particular. See Figure 2.

concerned, and is thus a transhistorical and transregional term used to refer to language(s) which, when written down, use 'Chinese' characters. But *Zhongwen* may refer to both oral and written Chinese; to the national language—*Guoyu* 國語, as it was called in the first half of the twentieth century, and as it is still called today on Taiwan—or *Putonghua* 普通, the 'common language', as it has been called since 1949 in the PRC. This national language or *lingua franca* is also based on northern Chinese. 'Mandarin' or 'Mandarin Chinese' is the term often used by non-Chinese to describe this national language, to distinguish it from Cantonese and other languages of China often mistakenly termed 'dialects'.[iii] *Zhongwen* would also cover the premodern written vernacular, *baihua* 白話 ('plain talk'), as well as the premodern literary language, *wenyanwen* 文言文.

In the PRC, Chinese is often referred to as *Hanyu* 漢語 ('Han language'). Again this may refer to oral or written Chinese, the language of the officially determined majority Han ethnicity, even though many within the Han ethnic category use another language such as Cantonese, *Minnanhua* 閩南話 (the language of Fujian and Taiwan), or *Wu* 吳 (the language of the Shanghai region). When referring to today's China, *Hanyu* is effectively modern standard Chinese (MSC), in other words *Putonghua* or what foreigners call Mandarin. But Hanyu may also refer to the premodern language, so the term is often qualified as *xiandai Hanyu* 現代漢語 ('modern Hanyu') as opposed to *gu* 古 or *gudai* 古代 ('ancient Hanyu'). But more on this modern/ancient divide later.

iii. Strictly speaking, 'Mandarin', or *guanhua* 官話—literally 'functionary-speak' or 'mandarin-talk'—refers only to the spoken language, since it served only as the oral *lingua franca* of the officials or Mandarins, *guan* 官話, who for written communication used the literary language, *wenyanwen* 文言文.

Huayu 華語 is often used to designate standard Chinese for a non-mainland Chinese or overseas Chinese public, who associate more readily with the idea of *Hua* than they do with *Han*. It is for instance used in Singapore to designate Modern Standard Chinese, and is found in the expression *Xinjiapo Huayu* 新加坡華語, or Singapore Mandarin.

'Chinese' may also refer to 'Chinese literature' just as 'English' may refer to 'English literature'. However, there are several terms in Modern Standard Chinese today. *Zhongguo wenxue* 中國文學, which sinologists translate as 'Chinese literature', literally means 'China literature' or 'literature of China'. This could be understood quite innocently—after all, we talk of British literature and American literature to distinguish between national literatures within the larger family of English literature, which many in any case still understand as pertaining to England, and perhaps Britain and Ireland. 'Literature in English' would be a more inclusive way of referring to the many literatures that exist in the English language. But just as the term 'British literature' would not evoke in most people's minds the use of Welsh and Gaelic as a literary language of Britain, so 'China literature' refers to literature in Chinese, and thus excludes literature of China in Tibetan, Uighur and other minority languages such as Korean.

Zhongguo wenxue is also used transhistorically, to refer to the literature written in the premodern language for more than 2,000 years, even though during those two millennia no writers ever referred to their writings as *Zhongguo wenxue*. To sum up, in the dominant collective imaginary, 'China literature' refers to literature written in 'Chinese' characters, within the space that is now China, in either modern Chinese or the premodern vernacular or in the premodern 'literary' language *wenyan* 文言; but it excludes what is written in languages such as Tibetan. There is, however, also a specific term for literature written in

Hanyu (the language of the Han) written down in *Hanzi* 漢字 ('Chinese characters'), and that is *Hanwen wenxue* 漢文文學, or 'literature in Han writing', where *Hanwen* 漢文 (Han writing) refers to the written language from the Han dynasty onwards.

The term *Hanwen* is also used to specify language written in characters as opposed to Romanized script. During the Republican period (1912–49) there existed projects to spell out characters in the Latin alphabet not merely as an aid to learning them, but so as to replace them altogether. Indeed, abandoning characters, in order to universalize the use of a national standard language, was seriously considered by intellectuals and the political authorities. In the years just after the 1911 Chinese Revolution, the prominent intellectual Hu Shi 胡適 (1891–1962) discussed in his diary the question of 'Whether or not our country's language can become a language using letters', and concluded that the abandonment of characters was not desirable: 'The reason Han writing [writing in characters] is difficult to popularize lies not in Han writing itself, but in the imperfect way it is taught'.[2]

Hu Shi distinguishes between 'letters' (*zimu* 字母) and 'Han writing' (*Hanwen*); and, writing in 1915, he still expresses himself in the old literary language (*wenyan*), rather than the modern, national vernacular he advocated. It is also noteworthy that he refers to 'our country's language' *wo guo yu* 吾國語, refraining from referring to 'Chinese' with use of *Zhongwen* or any of the other ways we have seen to describe Chinese language or literature. Today, a century later, 'letters' are confined to the pinyin Romanization system, used merely as an aid to identifying the pronunciation of characters and in representing names in foreign language texts. There is no further discussion of using the Latin alphabet to replace characters.[iv]

iv. Hanyu *Pinyin* Romanization is the official romanization system of the

All of the terms explored above translate into English as simply 'China' or 'Chinese'. It is easily understandable how simple it is to mask, intentionally or unintentionally, the complexity of the lexicon. When translating from Chinese into English, everything becomes 'China' or 'Chinese'; but when we attempt to translate from English or other languages into Chinese, what becomes obvious is the extent to which these two terms are extremely reductive of the diverse and complex political and historical issues foregrounded by the process of translation. In short, the English subsumes a host of historically, geopolitically and ethnically distinct significations.

People's Republic of China. Developed in the 1950s, it has been used to represent Chinese names in foreign-language publications since the end of the 1970s. Thus, Mao Tse-tung became Mao Zedong, Chou En-lai became Zhou Enlai. It was preceded by several other systems, mainly developed by missionaries and sinologists, which aimed to spell out and represent the written language. While pinyin works fairly well in rendering the sounds of *Putonghua* (the 'common standard language'), throughout China many speakers of the language pronounce the sounds quite differently. Pinyin is discussed further below.

2

ZHONGGUO AND THE HISTORIC VOCABULARY OF NATIONALISM

As for older historical uses of the term *zhongguo* 中國, the sinologist Wolfgang Behr has succinctly traced the usages and semantic possibilities in his work on premodern translation.[1] The term *zhongguo* is found as early as the Western Zhou dynasty 西周 (1046–771 BCE) on a bronze inscription excavated in 1963 and dating from around 1042–06 BCE.[2] Behr translates *zhongguo* 中國 in this context as 'the central states'; he also suggests the meanings 'capital' and 'royal domain'. The centralization of multifarious, vying states did not occur before 221 BCE, when the homogenizing Qin dynasty imposed itself militarily.[i] Before that, multiple vassal states coexisted around a principal or dominant state, which was more a fortified city-state or *yi* 邑 where the dominant sovereign raised his banner or *zhong* 中, 'a symbol of the centrality of the royal domain'. This central state became known as the *zhongguo* 中國. Under the Eastern Zhou 東周 (770–221 BCE), the term became associated with the central states as a whole, distinct from the barbarian 'outside world'. But at no point until the modern era was there a direct correlation between *zhongguo* 中國 and the West's 'China'.

i. Beyond historical reality, it was Mao Zedong's championing of the Qin monarch's achievements in the 1960s that made the Qin dynasty loom large in the popular imaginary.

As to the terms employing the character Han 漢 / 汉, Behr traces *hanzu* 漢族—which today would translate as 'Han ethnicity'—to the end of the Northern Wei Dynasty 北魏 (386–534 CE), but only in the sense of 'Han clansman'.[3] *Hanren* 漢人 in the sense of 'Han people' occurs in Sima Qian's *Shiji* 史記, known in English as *Records of the Grand Historian* (second century BCE).[4] As for expressions relating to the language, in the mid-fourth century CE, we find *Hanyan* 漢言 in the Annals of the Later Han *Hou Han Ji* 後漢紀; and *Hanyu* 漢語 in the *Nan Qi Shu* 南齊書 (537 CE). Both of these terms may be translated as 'Han language'.[ii] 'Han' language, then, was quite simply the language used by the court and the administration of the Han sovereigns and their successors over the succeeding millennia; it cannot anachronistically be called a national language. It was the written literary language that unified the bureaucracy, and the medium of an elite written culture throughout the territory ruled over by the dynastic powers at any given time. Let us recall that all functionaries were 'men of letters', and that to become a Mandarin a mastery of the written culture was essential.

Even when foreigners took over the reins of the state, as was most notably the case with the Mongol Yuan dynasty (1271–1368 CE) and the Manchu Qing (1644–1911 CE), the written language that had served the philosophers Confucius, Laozi 老子 and Zhuangzi 莊子 remained the language of bureaucratic communication and elite cultural expression. However, the twentieth-century Republic needed, as all nation-states do, a unifying, homogenized language accessible to the greatest number. Only for a brief moment at the beginning of the 1912

ii. After the brief rule of the Qin dynasty (221–206 BCE), which so efficiently unified the territory and standardized weights, measures, coinage, transport, and, not least, writing systems, the Han consolidated and extended this unified polity over a period of four centuries (206 BCE–220 CE).

Republic was the written language what would come to be known as *gudai Hanyu* 古代漢語, literally 'old-time Han language', or what is commonly known in English as 'classical Chinese'. It was rapidly succeeded by *kuo-yü* or *guoyu* 國語 or the 'national language', a kind of written-down version of the oral lingua franca that was Mandarin.

The later use of the term Han, signifying the dominant ethnic group and its language, is an affair of the twentieth century; the category 'Han nationality'—'*Han minzu*' 漢民族, a homogeneous, unified Han ethnic entity—was 'an entirely modern phenomenon', invented to facilitate the creation of a nation-state. It achieved 'its greatest popularity under [China's first President] Dr. Sun Yat-sen.'[5] We should also recall that, in the Cantonese-speaking region of the south, the region annexed to what is now China under the Tang Dynasty (618–907 CE), the populace refer to themselves as *Tangren* 唐人 or 'Tang people' rather than Han, despite being officially classified by the authorities as ethnically Han.

As to the naming of the form of state ruled over by a paramount sovereign, Western observers and scholars would call it the 'Empire'; but, once again, the name and conception of empire did not exist. The sovereign, inheritor of the mandate of heaven, *tianming* 天命, simply reigned supreme over the entire, 'civilized' world, that which was under the heavens, or 'under the sky' (*tianxia* 天下).[iii] So this was not an empire in any European sense, and, as we have seen, the state that Westerners called 'China' existed neither nominally nor conceptually. This state, ruled by a succession of dynastic houses, was what

iii. Indeed, the late nineteenth-century/early twentieth-century 'nationalist' revolutionary Sun Yat-sen's democratizing slogan was *tianxia wei gong* 天下為公, 'all under the sky for the public'—'all under the sky' meaning everything under the Manchu sky, and implying the need for emancipation from Manchu rule.

Europeans would call the 'Chinese Empire', or quite simply 'China', but was both a space and a time before China as such, predating the imagining of China in the nineteenth century. It was what I call China-Before-China. China proper, China the modern nation-state—a really existing China with a shared, global, national consciousness—is entirely an affair of the twentieth and twenty-first centuries. All the rest is invention, reinvention and anachronistic projection back into the past: a modern vision of 'history' that serves the present.

In the nineteenth century, the proper noun *Zhongguo* 中國 came into use, in reaction to colonial aggression—to what is innocently and unthinkingly called China's 'encounter' with West, as if 'China' happened to bump into the West while out for a stroll. When using the term, some may have been imagining the land of the Han last governed by the Ming, but for foreigners such as the British, *Zhongguo* referred to the territory governed by the Manchu dynasty, the *Daqing* 大清 or Great Qing, and in this sense it started to be used by the literati; the proto-intellectuals of the nineteenth century. We find *Zhongguo* alongside 'China' in the unequal treaties, and notably in the Nanjing Treaty drawn up by the British after the First Opium War and signed on 29 August 1842. While the two signatory states are given as *Da Qingguo* 大清國 (Great Qing) and *Da Yingguo* 大英國 (Great Britain), the term *Zhongguo* 中國 also occurs in the treaty a total of eight times, to designate a nation imagined and identified by the British as 'China'.

We have already seen how translation leads to conflation of meanings, and this may be further illustrated in Fairbank's and Teng's translation of the 1905 'Manifesto of the *Tongmenghui* 同盟會宣布', the revolutionary movement that campaigned for the overthrow of the Manchu dynasty. The Manifesto, with its four-point strategy, was a key text in the conceptual model of the yearned-for republic, a founding text or blueprint against which the resultant Chinese state would later be judged.[iv] It was drawn up by the future first president of the Republic of China, Sun Yat-sen 孫逸仙 (1866–1925), also known as Sun Zhongshan 孫中山.[6] Let us take a closer look. Fairbank and Teng translated the opening of Sun's first point into English thus:

> 1) *Drive out the Tartars*. The Manchus of today were originally the eastern barbarians beyond the Great Wall. They frequently caused border troubles during the Ming dynasty; then when China was in a disturbed state they came inside Shanhaikuan, conquered China, and enslaved our Chinese people. Those who opposed them were killed by the hundreds of thousands, and our Chinese have been a people without a nation for two hundred and sixty years.

Here is the original text:

> 驅除韃虜。今之满洲, 本塞外东胡, 昔在明朝 , 屡為邊患; 後乘中國多事, 長驅入关, 滅我中國, 据我政府, 迫我漢人為其奴隶, 有不從者, 殺戳億萬 。我漢人為亡國之民者二百六十年於斯!

The text is in 'literary Chinese' and so gives greater latitude when translating into English than modern standard Chinese. While Sun twice uses the word *Zhongguo* 中國, translated here as 'China', what Fairbank and Teng give as 'enslaved our Chinese

iv. Founding principles, such as the French republican motto *Liberté, Égalité, Fraternité*, are the building blocks of what political theorist Cornelius Castoriadis calls the 'instituting imaginary': the original blueprint of a national community. What practically results from this blueprint is called the 'instituted imaginary'. When the gap between the two becomes too great, popular confidence breaks down and a new 'imaginary' must be devised. When this gap appeared in the early Chinese Republic, student contestation, warlord domination and attempted monarchic restoration ended in civil war between nationalists and Communists that ultimately resulted in a new imaginary: the People's Republic of China.

people' would be more accurately translated as 'pressed our Han people into slavery', the original specifically mentioning Hanren 漢人. Similarly, the last sentence should be: 'Our Han people have been the populace of a perished country for 260 years.' But the translators have chosen to employ the modern vocabulary of the nation-state; the Han become 'the Chinese' and the 'Chinese … a people without a nation', whereas the original refers to the Han as the people or populace of a 'destitute', 'ruined' or 'perished' *country* or *state*, the sense that *wangguo* 亡國 had for over two millennia in the literary language.

Here is the text of Point 1 again (emphasis added):

> 1) *Drive out the Tartars*. The Manchus of today were originally the eastern barbarians beyond the Great Wall. They frequently caused border troubles during the Ming dynasty; then when China was in a disturbed state they came inside Shanhaikuan, conquered China, and enslaved our *Chinese people*. Those who opposed them were killed by the hundreds of thousands, and *our Chinese* have been a people without a *nation* for two hundred and sixty years.

In the above translation, the word 'Chinese' is used twice to refer to the population. In the original, in my translation below (emphasis added), it does not occur at all. There is also no mention of the equivalent for 'nation':

> 1) Drive out the Tartars. Today's Manchus were Eastern Barbarians outside the current frontiers. Formerly during the Ming dynasty, they repeatedly menaced the borderlands. Later when China was in a disturbed state, they penetrated Shanhaiguan [the terminus of the Great Wall that adjoins the sea], snuffed out our China, took over our government, pressed our *Han people* into slavery. As for those who refused to submit, they were slaughtered in their thousands and

> millions. *We Han* have been the people of a defeated *country* for the past two hundred and sixty years.

That Sun had already adopted the vocabulary necessary to his instituting imaginary of a Chinese republic is undeniable. However, the original text, written in the old literary language of the bureaucracy, is not yet imbued with the nationalist language of an instituted, or extant, nation-state or republic. Again the nuance of the original is masked or even reduced by the translation into English some fifty years later, after the foundation of the current PRC. In this first point, Sun Yat-sen is making a stark distinction between Han and Manchu; the word for nation does not occur; and while the text mentions China, it makes no mention of Chinese. In Sun's second point there is a shift into a comprehensive nationalist discourse replete with anachronistic terms, calling up a sovereign, Han-ruled nation-state:

> 2) *Restore China.* China is the China of the Chinese. The government of China should be in the hands of the Chinese. After driving out the Tartars we must restore our national state…

恢復中華。中國者, 中國人之中國, 中國之政治, 中國人任之, 驅除韃虜之後, 光復我民族的國家

Here the translation more or less accurately represents Sun's political slippage from Han to Chinese; the Han are no longer singled out, but have given way to the Chinese of *Zhongguo* 中國. 'Restore *Zhonghua*' starts point 2, as if *Zhonghua* had already existed before the Manchus; that is, before 1644—as if their reign constituted a mere hiatus. And what the translator gives as 'we must restore our national state' is rather 'recover/reconstitute the (nation) state of our ethnicity/race.'[7] In either case, the implication is that a return to the status quo before the

1644 Manchu invasion and occupation would simply entail a 'return' to a pre-existing 'Chineseness'. But, merely in terms of territory, the state boundaries the Republic of China inherited from the Manchus exceeded anything that a non-foreign sovereign had ever ruled over. Indeed, the 'geographical instantiation of the modern Chinese state involved … a highly problematic legacy from the Qing', not least because the Manchu expansion had brought within its bounds several large ethnic groups and their homelands.[8] These included Tibet and Mongolia, all the territory in between Lhasa and the Gobi Desert, and of course what would become known as Manchuria. Not since the Mongol khans of the short-lived Yuan dynasty (1271–1368 CE) had these territories briefly been ruled by dynastic sovereigns. The surface area governed by the Ming stood at 2.5 million square miles, while that passed down by the Qing in 1911 covered 4.4 million; for comparison, the surface area of the USA today is 3.5 million square miles.

Moreover, relative prosperity had brought about a further demographic change in the Manchu era: a huge rise in population figures. The expansion of the frontiers alone did not account for this explosion, since the populace was mainly concentrated in the space previously controlled by the Ming, and not in the newly acquired territories. In the mid-seventeenth century, the population of the Ming lands stood at somewhere between 160 and 175 million.[9] When the Qing collapsed in 1911 and gave way to the Republic, the population was over 400 million, and this despite the cumulative impact on the economy of the Opium Wars, rebellions, and mass emigration.[10] These were the geographic, ethnic and demographic foundations of the new, really existing, 'China'.

In the fourth point of Sun Yat-sen's manifesto, 'Equalize land ownership' or 'Equalize land rights' 平均地權, the term *guojia* 國家 refers to the state, while *guomin* 國民 is translated by

Teng and Fairbank as 'people of the nation'; more usual translations would be 'citizen' for the noun and 'national' for the adjective. As a southerner, a Cantonese-speaker, and a returned diasporic subject (he was born in Guangdong but spent his adolescence in Hawaii), Sun Yat-sen's identity was itself ambiguous. Similarly many of the revolutionaries were from the largely Cantonese-speaking Guangdong province, which 'hosted' the foreign colonies of Macao and Hong Kong, and so had experienced greater exposure to foreign imperialism and its culture; they were also far removed geographically from the northern heartland of the 'Mandarin-speaking' majority. Some decades later, in the elaboration of his 'Three Principles', Sun would significantly modify his concept of how the nation was composed, but at this moment in time, he needed to establish as wide a 'national' base as possible for his new republic. To do so, he adopted a discourse that not only assembled several 'ethnicities' into an imagined Chinese 'nation', but also one that glossed over linguistic and 'racial' differences.

In fact, there had been and there continued to be debate amongst the elite at the turn of the nineteenth and twentieth centuries over the contours and composition of the desired post-Manchu state. The more radical elements of those contesting the Qing Dynasty wanted the new nation-state to consist uniquely of the Han; the Manchus, considered alien, were to be excluded altogether from the imagined Chinese nation. The more moderate thinkers saw the Manchus, and others identified as non-Han peoples, as belonging to a broader 'national' family. In 1912, once the new state was established, all parties agreed to a Republic of Five Peoples or nationalities or *wuzu gonghe* 五族共和, represented by the five horizontal coloured bands of the national flag. Popularly known as the Five Colours Flag (*wuseqi* 五色旗), it served as the national flag from 1912 to 1924 and was intended to represent the 'five peoples [of China] united in harmony'.

From top to bottom, the colours were red (*Han* 漢), yellow (*Man* 滿 Manchu), blue (*Meng* 蒙 Mongolian), white (*Hui* 回 Muslim) and black (*Zang* 藏 Tibetan). The term *Hui* was used to refer to all Muslim and Islamic peoples, regardless of their ethnic or linguistic background, and was first institutionalized under the nationalist republican government.[v] These five peoples or nationalities were all said to belong to the *Zhonghua minzu* 中华民族 or 'Chinese nation', although, confusingly, *minzu* 民族 at the time also translated the English words 'race', 'nation' or 'people'. Thus a 'territorial conception of nationhood' became integral to the Chinese national imaginary.[11] This was even more the case when the Communists came to power in 1949, with their universalist Marxist-Leninist ideology, and expanded the number of 'peoples', ethnicities, or 'nationalities' to a total of fifty-six, including the Han.

Western notions of both 'race' and 'historiography' were necessary to historically justify the category *Zhongguoren* 中國人, so whether in order to include certain 'racial' or ethnic groups within the national family, or to exclude them the better to define Chineseness, Western 'scientific' categorizations were once again invoked. The vociferous reformer Liang Qichao 梁啟超 (1873–1929) adopted a Western historiographical approach. Rejecting the millennia-long dynastic regime of historical classification, he divided 'Chinese' history into three periods: ancient, medieval and modern. At the same time, Liang adapted Western anthropological theories of race, claiming in an essay on the relationship between race and history: 'There are historic peoples and non-historic peoples'[12] and that naturally the Chinese belonged to the historic peoples.[13]

v. Under the PRC, *Hui* acquired a more limited and specific usage, denoting 'only those Muslim peoples not distinguished by language and locality'. In Taiwan, the term is still used to refer to all Muslim peoples. See Gladney, *Muslim Chinese*, p. 30.

He drew up a table in which appear the 'yellow races' and the 'white races'. The category 'yellow' was divided into three subcategories: in the first were Chinese, Japanese, Korean, 'Siamese', and 'other East Asian peoples'; in the second category were Mongols, Tartars, and Tungu ('today's Siberians') and 'other North and Central Asian peoples'; in the third category we find Turks, Hungarians, and 'other people of Yellow race in Europe'.[14] Where we might expect to find *Han* in Liang's text for Chinese, we find instead *Zhongguoren*. Like the Japanese in the case of Japan, the Chinese 'people' or 'race' thus became synonymous with the national territory itself.[15]

By 1924, Sun Yat-sen had made fundamental and explicit the link between nation and race. In his 'Three Principles of the People' lectures, he made his case for the particular situation of *Zhongguo*, China, asserting that 'race' and 'nation' were one and the same:

> In China since the days of Ching [Qin] and Han, the country has been made up of one race; while in foreign countries, one race may form several states or one state may comprise several different races. The British Empire is made up of the white race as the principal people, and the black people, the brown people, and others. The statement, then, that the nationality is the nation-group cannot be applied to Great Britain.[16]

Sun's previous insistence on the Chinese nation being multiethnic or 'multi-racial' seemed to have now been elided. In line with contemporary, dominant theories of race, he added:

> The reason for this multiplicity of races may be summed up as natural forces; although difficult to analyse, the main force is 'heredity' [literally: blood system]. The reason for Chinese people's yellowness is simply due to our yellow heredity. The heredity of ancestors is forever transmitted down to a people, so the force of heredity is very great.[17]

Despite the official rhetoric of China being a multi-ethnic state, this notion of China consisting of a single race persists in the twenty-first century. During Donald Trump's state visit to China, as he was guided around the Forbidden City by Xi Jinping, the American president undiplomatically suggested that the world's oldest culture was Egypt's. The Chinese president, obliged to agree, retorted with the staid shibboleth:

> However, there is only China that has an uninterrupted culture. The way we look now is also the way earliest [Chinese] people looked. Black hair, yellow skin, passed down to us. We call ourselves successors of the Dragon.[18]

3

CHINA, ITS AUTHORITIES AND THE NATIONAL IMAGINARY

Today, the imagining, defining and recounting of 'China' is increasingly dominated by China's regnant authority and segments of the Chinese intellectual elite. Central government has fixed the objective of constructing and imposing an official standard version of 'China' to be propagated internationally. Yet, this is no yearned-for decolonization of the telling of China's story, nor is it a decolonization of the minds—were such a thing possible—of the inheritors of those intellectuals who, for over a century, have sought to construct and invent China using Western paradigms, hybridized or not. No, the authorities and their agents frequently dress up this China as the 'natural' descendant and inheritor of an ancient and eternal China; indeed, this story of China's origins is to be found in the first line of the 'Preamble' to the Constitution of the People's Republic of China: 'China is a country with one of the longest histories in the world. The people of all of China's nationalities have jointly created a culture of grandeur....'[1]

And yet this now-official Chinese version of the national in large part coincides with or indeed recuperates a history concocted by Western sinologists. It was and remains what we may call an imaginary. Indeed, the Chinese who internalize and re-transmit this Orientalist vision of China are simply recycling an old Western conception of a long dreamt, and dreamt-up, China that does not represent the society and culture of today, but rather those of a nebulous, yet supposedly homogeneous, historical 'China', shimmering in the halcyon light of a fabulous, undifferentiated past, like a scene from Tolkien: Middle Kingdom as Middle Earth.

Indeed, it is this Orientalist 'China' whose identity and specificity were invented. That there is a past to what we have known in the West as China, Tartary, the Celestial Empire, Middle Kingdom and so on, I do not put in question. What does have to be seriously questioned, however, is the premodern existence of a culturally and societally homogeneous and monolithic 'China' which somehow naturally gave rise to the contemporary, harmonious and homogenized China desired and narrated by China's regnant power. This is a China which, the authorities would have us believe, is the 'natural', inevitable and destined inheritor of the march of 'Chinese' history, stretching back many millennia. It is this China that is purveyed to the world beyond. It is this 'Chinese dream' which now eschews the 'contamination' of Chinese society by the outside world.

The irony in this early-twenty-first century vision is that almost everything constitutive of today's China has come from the West, both the economic logic applied in China today and the accompanying technological/technical system, as Jacques Ellul has called the regime that has dominated the world for the past half-century. For Ellul, the 'technical' does not simply refer to objects, machines and industrial processes, but also comprises division of labour, professional training, government and politics, and organization of sports, leisure and health. It is, simply, the quest for the 'best way'. In this book, then, the 'technological' also refers to a technical system, wherein each aspect of human life is subject to control, manipulation, observation and experimentation, in the aim of arriving at demonstrable efficiency everywhere. The dominance of technology has been one result of this global order, as is clear to see today in China and the West alike.[i]

While Xi Jinping's 'Chinese dream' may have been a new iteration of a desired identitarian nation-state, the Chinese Communist Party is adept in the art of passing off the past as the present. The pretence that 'China always was' has been promoted by the authorities of the People's Republic of China since its inception in 1949. In conversation with a group of foreign visitors in 1964, in the build-up to the Cultural Revolution that would debunk Confucius, Mao Zedong famously declared:

> Confucius had a few good things in his favour, but still was not very good. We believe in speaking justly. Qin Shi Huang was much greater than Confucius. Confucius was full of empty talk. Qin Shi Huang was the first person to unify China [*Zhongguo*]. But not only did he unify China politically, he also unified China's writing system, unified all sorts of standards such as weights and measures, there are several such standards that are still in use today. Amongst China's past feudal monarchs there was no-one who surpassed him. But he was cursed for thousands of years. They cursed him for two reasons: he killed 460 intellectuals; he burnt a few books.[2]

Mao clearly identified himself with the dynastic unifier Qin Shi Huang, and when the Cultural Revolution (1966–76) was launched two years later, many more than 460 would be killed; the book-burning would take on huge proportions. Although Mao dissociated his revolution from feudal China, he still felt

i. Until the last quarter of the twentieth century, there was a clear semantic distinction between 'technical' (*la technique, technicien*) and 'technological' (*la technologie, technologique*), but since then the sense of 'technical' has been absorbed by the now-broader 'technological'. Ellul himself came to accept this conflation. See Ellul, *Le Système technicien*, p. 93.

the need to use a specific part of the past to bolster his own present vision of China. The unifying, homogenizing, centralizing force that the Qin emperor represented is what appealed to Mao. Yet, Mao had no time for the Confucian tradition and the past it had propped up. Like the Legalist philosophers who traduced Confucius and bolstered Qin Shi Huang two millennia before, Mao placed the present, and himself, above the past. In his 1936 poem *Snow*, he wrote:

And Genghis Khan,
Proud Son of Heaven for a day,
Knew only shooting eagles, bow outstretched
All are past and gone!
For truly great men
Look to this age alone.

While the 'China' story the PRC's authorities wished and wish to diffuse may be fictive and fantastic, the China that has thus been created over the past century is real enough. The reality of China as it exists today is the instituted imaginary,[ii] whose instituting imaginary was created at the turn of the nineteenth and twentieth centuries and which has been inflected and re-created at various moments—notably in 1949, in 1978 and again in the early 1990s—and now reinforced under President Xi (2012–).

China the nation-state, whose institutional inception followed the overthrow of the Manchu dynasty, may be seen as having traversed a long moment of nation creation, and as the instituting of an initial, idealistic imaginary based on an already re-invented past—one we saw in the manifestos of the 'Father of the Nation', Sun Yat-sen. Subsequent to the mid-nineteenth-century 'Opium Wars', China's military-technological, especially maritime, 'backwardness' had become

ii. See Chapter 2, n. iv.

suddenly apparent, and jolted part of China's elite into initiating reforms in favour of Westernization and 'self-reinforcement'. These efforts were renewed by the Reform Movement of 1898, and confirmed in the post-Versailles 4 May Movement of 1919.[iii/3]

However, we may also see this century-long history as a succession of flawed, failed and incessantly relaunched nation-building projects. While the founding imaginary dates from before the 1911 revolution, its legal institution dates from 1912 and its cultural institution from the young intellectual elite's agitation in the 1920s. As Castoriadis has shown, when the gap between an 'instituting' imaginary (such as the ideals of liberty, equality and fraternity behind the French revolution) and the 'instituted' imaginary (the lived reality of French people) becomes too great for a community to sustain, a rupture will result and a new imaginary will be called for. This is what occurred in China in 1919. The instituting imaginary of the Chinese nation-state, which we can date back to the late nineteenth century, resulted in an instituted imaginary far removed from the ideals of the early twentieth. It was in 1919–20 that a newly inflected imaginary—one that foregrounded linguistic and cultural transformation—was instituted with the expansion of the New Culture Movement, which saw increasing unity among intellectuals; invigorated social and political programmes promoted by the New Youth Society's flagship magazine *Xinqingnian* 新青年 (*La Jeunesse*); and renewed calls for an iconoclastic rupture with the past.[4] John Dewey, the American educationalist and epistemologist much admired by Chinese intellectuals, commented on the student movement in 1921:

> Their burden was the need of educational change; attacks upon the family system; discussion of socialism; of democratic ideas;

iii. *Yangwu yundong, ziqiang yundong* 洋務運動,自強運動.

> of all kinds of utopias … Lacking definite background, the students thought all ideas and proposals much alike, provided only they were new and involved getting away from old customs and traditions.[5]

Then came the Communist take-over, or 'Liberation', in 1949. A new Communist nation-building imaginary, which commanded widespread support and enthusiasm, was instituted. But by the end of the 1950s this new nation-building force revealed itself to be a chimera, thinly veiling state repression and conservatism. The Great Proletarian Cultural Revolution (*Wuchanjieji wenhua da geming* 无产阶级文化大革命) that followed could be seen as a hiatus in the nation-building process, effectively halted by factional in-fighting. Industrial and infrastructural modernization was indeed curbed, and yet the processes of linguistic and cultural homogenization were deepened further, with the production, recording and nationwide distribution of 'revolutionary spectacles' and their spin-offs.

Deng Xiaoping's emphatic return to power in 1978 constituted a reinvigoration of the 1949 Communist version of the national(ist) imaginary, in which all sectors of the population invested their hopes; and many expected political reforms and freedoms to accompany economic, pro-capitalist reforms. In the early years of Deng Xiaoping's consolidation of power, such was indeed the optimistic horizon that was promised. However, the numerous mini-campaigns against 'bourgeois liberalization' during the 1980s also signalled that the final arbiter would always remain the centralized power of the regnant Communist Party.

During the spring events of 1989 leading up to the Tiananmen massacre, the reintroduction of the original 1919 revolutionary demand for democracy constituted a divergence from the official Communist imaginary instituted by the post-Mao apparatus. This dissident desire for a differently configured future, expressed by numerous elements within society demanding the autonomy they had dared to imagine theirs, ended with the 4 June 1989 Tiananmen massacre. Subsequently, in the 1990s, the promise of social and individual autonomy was subtracted from the Communists' project, and replaced by Deng Xiaoping's economistic, materialist project—vigorously promoted by the political apparatus of an authoritarian state in which heteronomy, and not autonomy, held sway.

We may, then, see the twentieth century as a series of attempts to institute divergent national imaginaries. And yet, today, most Chinese people still adhere to the imaginary the rulers have imposed, through ideology and economic inducement—despite the failure, so far, of this officially projected imaginary to provide individual and societal autonomy, or even the most basic political rights. A list of issues would include the creation of an underclass of ex-peasant migrant workers deprived of full socio-economic rights, the failure to address the political claims of ethnic minorities, the exclusion of Tibetans and Uighurs from decision-making regarding the economic use and abuse of their territories' resources, more recently the cavalier treatment of Hong Kongers' demands for legitimate, democratic control over their lives, and indeed the lack of political rights for all of China's citizens. This is to leave aside—but for how much longer can we afford to do so?—the ecological catastrophe and widespread danger to public health brought about by pollution and disregard for safety standards. This situation has been exacerbated by the authorities' unthinking adhesion to the global technological-economic system, in their attempt to accumulate wealth and maintain hegemony within China, to expand their presence in the region, and to see the country's interests maintained in the rest of the world.

And yet, we might leave aside the Taiwanese, Hong Kongers, Tibetans and Uighurs, who, I suggest, have never in their majority subscribed to the dominant Chinese nationalist imaginaries put forward over the past century—how could they be expected to? Without them, a huge number of China's citizens are still invested in a sometimes extreme nationalist imaginary, despite all the negative factors that weigh on the individual and the community in the twenty-first century.

All in all, we can discern a collective nationalist imaginary flowing like metaphoric magma through the twentieth century, with its layers of successive and supplementary social significations—sometimes active, sometimes suspended, but still contributing to the whole, sliding hegemonically into the middle of the twenty-first century.[iv/6]

iv. I understand 'magma' perhaps more literally than Castoriadis: as a complex of significations in perpetual, molten, movement, sliding through time and space, retaining the old agglomerate but acquiring new matter in its mixture of significations. Or perhaps Castoriadis also intended this.

4

WOMEN IN NATIONALISM'S SNARE

Women's status in 'traditional' society was low. In the Confucian 'six relations', man features as 'father', 'elder brother', 'younger brother' and 'son', whereas woman only features as 'mother' and 'wife'. In the turn-of-the-century agitation for a new society, it was in the interest of young, literate women of the emergent bourgeoisie to side with the revolutionary tendencies of the intellectual class that was in the making. Young men saw their only route to autonomy in the dismantling of Confucian ideology that protected and promoted patriarchal hierarchy; how much more so did elite women, for if the kinship hierarchy placed the father above the sons who owed him obeisance, daughters occupied an even lowlier position. In a world dominated by Confucian ideology, which favoured female seclusion, women's possibilities of a life outside the home were socially limited to 'lower-class outsiders' occupying such roles as nuns, matchmakers, or female healers.[1]

These marginally literate women at least enjoyed a certain mobility, compared to the house-bound women of the gentry to whom they provided services, although even such limited, minor social roles were resented by professional men.[2] Starting in the eighteenth century, elite women increasingly had access to learning and culture. Some won fame for their poetry, especially in the cities of Hangzhou, Suzhou and Guangzhou, where there was a preponderance of leading female writers and artists.[3] Under the Ming (1368–1644), women painters in the main had been courtesans, while the 'majority of famous women painters active after 1700, in fact, were married women with children'.[4] Nevertheless, even upper-class women were seriously disadvantaged, and there were 'clear contrasts between the education of sons and the education of daughters in a world of strict gender segregation':

> First, all daughters, regardless of class, were educated to work and to procreate in the service of a male line. Bound feet, reproduction, and work kept daughters close to home … A young girl first served her mother, training to be a future daughter-in-law. Then she served her mother-in-law by waiting on the older woman's personal needs and bearing the sons of the next generation … Women who became brides and mothers entered a descent group in which they were expected to prepare the rites of ancestor worship in the home'.[5]

Thus, before marrying, upper-class women had the time to write, but once they had become mothers their talents were channelled into 'the work and rituals of domestic life'.[6] As for women of other social classes, even in the late nineteenth century, they were mostly illiterate.

At the dawn of the twentieth century, then, women had a great deal to gain from the overturning of the patriarchal order. However, elite men's attitudes to the participation of women in the creation of China the nation-state were ambiguous. The persistence of a hierarchically gendered ideology amongst those elite young men demanding democracy is betrayed in a 1906 'First Draft Programme of the Alliance of Students in Shanghai from All Provinces', which laid out the 'national aspirations' of students in the emerging modern metropolis of Shanghai. Their main demands were for a national language, expanded educational opportunities and more translations of foreign works. In their list of twelve aims, the tenth was 'To encourage schools for women in order to train teachers for kindergartens'.[7] In a sense, this was a 'natural' perpetuation of the role of women in elite society, since in premodern times 'many elite sons received their early classical lessons from their mothers' as part of their early preparation for the civil service examinations.[8]

And yet, at the turn of the century, elite women activists and writers, the most celebrated of whom was Qiu Jin 秋瑾 (1875–1907), made valiant efforts to challenge women's acceptance of a subjugation that stemmed from their having 'internalized inherited gender ideologies'. At the same time they pushed for the nationalist agenda, in which they saw the 'salvation' of women.[9] Some feminist scholars are sympathetic towards the women who invested in the nationalist discourse 'with its attendant concepts of national salvation [*jiuguo* 救國], citizenship [*guomin* 國民], [and] human rights [*renquan* 人權]', and who saw it as constituting 'an enabling force'. Other feminist critics point to the 'nationalist inflection' in women's writing and journalism 'as evidence of the limits and constraints on feminist discourse of this period'.[10] Tellingly, in the year of her demise, Qiu Jin established one of the first magazines to espouse women's rights, entitled *Zhongguo nü bao* 中國女報: literally 'China woman periodical'.

In the early years of the Republic, the hopes of pioneering intellectual women were dashed:

> Despite Sun Yat-sen's having promised otherwise, the National Assembly [of the new republic] refused to recognize the principle of female equality or women's right to vote … With Yuan Shikai's [袁世凱] presidency such goals became all the more remote: in 1913 he officially banned women from joining

political associations, attending political events, and contributing to radical publications. Such measures did not put a halt to feminist activism; they did, however, put a considerable damper on hopes that the 'new' China would usher in better conditions for Chinese women.[11]

It was in the sphere of literature, in which a great number of women were active, that the debate played out on China's 'New Woman', and yet even magazines purporting to advance the cause of women were often controlled by men. The 1920 'Xin funü xuanyan' 新婦女宣言 (Manifesto of the New Woman), which appeared on the first page of the first issue of *New Woman* magazine (*Xin funü*), 'outlined the modern Chinese New Woman, a figure expected to devote herself to realiz[ing] social change, to sacrific[ing] herself for women's future emancipation and China's freedom from both tradition and foreign imperialist aggression'.[12] Such a vision did not really upset the patriarchal order in which woman existed to serve others. Male reformers, while wanting women to reject feudal ideology, nevertheless wanted them to adopt moderate Western role models; women who put the national, revolutionary interest above a more specifically feminist agenda:

> Their imagination of the New Woman was one who devoted herself to national salvation (in whatever political order) to eliminate women's social oppression for good. Ways in which women could be emancipated borrowed from foreign treatises on women's emancipation, such as those by Friedrich Engels, August Bebel, John Stuart Mill, Margaret Sanger, Alexandra Kollontai, and Yosano Akiko.[13]

Indeed, from the beginning of the twentieth century, the history of representation of women in both male- and female-authored literary and cultural texts demonstrates the recuperation and assimilation of feminist agendas by nation-oriented, male-dominated politics. The general revolution's claim to render futile the feminist revolution is not unique to China, but Chinese Communist culture has been particularly avid in subjugating feminist politics. Lu Tonglin forcefully historicizes and contextualizes this problem by referring to two iconic plays, one foreign, and one Chinese, 'that have characterized women's positions in the two major revolutions of twentieth-century China':

> Ibsen's *A Doll's House* and Tian Han's *The White-Haired Girl*. The former inspired the May Fourth generation to dream of a Chinese woman liberated from her traditional ties to kinship in the image of a Western individualistic middle-class woman; the latter represented the salvation of the oppressed peasant woman by the Communist Party. Between and beyond these two plays, other attempts have been made to 'save' Chinese women...[14]

Salvation, 'be it Christian, socialist, or revolutionary, implies a hierarchy', and women, 'after being saved symbolically and glamorously, finally always return to the bottom rung of a new hierarchy'.[15]

As for the screen, in the so-called progressive cinema of the 1930s and 1940s, which was sympathetic to the Communist Party, the particularity of women's concerns was habitually absorbed into a more general, universal project. In the 1934 silent film *Tiyu huanghou* 體育皇后, ('The Sports Queen'), scripted and directed by Sun Yu 孫瑜, a talented female athlete savours her individual success for a time, before being made to understand by a patriotic, progressive male trainer that sacrificing personal glory to the collective project is the preferable course. At a metaphorical level, the film is about constructing the national body by building healthy, athletic, disciplined female bodies.

By the eve of the founding of the PRC, the role and place of women is made even clearer in the film made by Chen Liting 陳鯉庭, *Liren xing* 麗人行, ('Ballad of the Beauties'), an adaptation of the 1933 film *Sange modeng nüxing* 三個摩登女性 (Three Modern Women). Set in 1944 Japanese-occupied Shanghai, the film stressed national unity at a moment, 1949, when the civil war was raging and the Communists' concern was to retain as much patriotic talent as possible for the task of reconstruction that lay ahead. Three women are portrayed: a working-class woman who is raped at the start of the film by drunken Japanese soldiers; a bourgeois woman who, despite being married to a collaborationist banker, is shown as having patriotic sentiments; and an educated, intellectual, progressive woman. In the resistance against the Japanese, the women are allowed to throw propaganda leaflets from Shanghai rooftops while the men hurl bombs.

The male lead, played by the 1930s star Zhao Dan 趙丹, is the former husband of the bourgeois woman, with whom he has a child. When the daughter is called upon to choose between the revolutionary father and the bourgeois mother, she chooses the father.

The rape of the working-class woman is analogous to the 'rape' of China, and thus is meant to incite the spectator to patriotic indignation rather than sympathy for the women thus treated. While what was visually foregrounded is the rape of a woman, the heavy subtext was that China's national honour had been besmirched. Woman here was, at best, standing in for the nation.

When women took the representation of their sex into their own hands, the depiction could be very different. Of the writers of the prerevolutionary period, that is before the 1949 Communist take-over of China, the most exceptional were those whose writing put the expression of female subjecthood before the dominant, nationalist, universalist ideology. In this sense their writing was unique, for few male writers forsook the nationalist narrative, even when contesting Communist literary doctrine. A handful of women writers were thus responsible for an alternative vision of Chinese modernity, one seen from a woman's perspective. The pantheon of such writers would include Xiao Hong 蕭紅 (1911–42), Ling Shuhua 凌叔華 (1900–90) and Eileen Chang 张爱玲 (1920–95). The latter two also wrote in English and spent their later years in exile, Ling Shuhua in England and Eileen Chang in California. Both were relatively neglected by the literary establishment and were only 'rediscovered' in the 1990s. These were not just good women writers; their stories and novels, eschewing the politics of the nation in favour of the politics of the personal, were quite simply ahead of their time. As such, they may be considered the most important writers writing in Chinese in their time. In 1961, the renowned scholar C.T. Hsia said this of Eileen Chang: 'Eileen Chang is not only the best and most important writer in Chinese today; her short stories alone invite comparison with, and in some cases superiority over, the work of serious modern women writers in English: Katherine Mansfield, Katherine Anne Porter, Eudora Welty, and Carson McCullers.'[16]

However, by the time Hsia wrote those words, China had become a closed society, and Chang's works censored by the Communist authorities. The situation in the West was little different; in Europe and North America, the vast majority of those responsible for teaching modern Chinese literature were sympathetic to the Maoist regime and its literary canon, and C.T. Hsia himself was derided. As Hsia remarked in what is now seen as a seminal essay, 'Obsession with China', what distinguished Republican-era Chinese literature was 'its obsessive concern with China as a nation afflicted with a spiritual disease and therefore unable to strengthen itself or change its set ways of inhumanity.'[17]

Later, under the Communist Party's post-1949 'New China', the national, universalist revolutionary ideology completely subsumed the feminist agenda. Lu Tonglin has remarked that 'Chinese women's representational power in the discourse of the Communist Party, instead of helping them make a break away from traditional gender discrimination, is currently used as an excuse by some intellectuals in China or in the field of Chinese studies overseas to formulate a misogynistic discourse in the post-Mao era'; a discourse underlying 'both traditional Confucian and modern communist ideologies in China':

> Both ideologies are, in the final analysis, essentially patriarchal. The intricate relationships of ideological and social forces further complicate the gender situation in contemporary China. However, this complexity ... may prevent us as feminist scholars in the West from falling into the same trap as did Chinese women in their aborted emancipation movement.[18]

5

ILLITERACY AND THE CULTURAL IMAGINARY

What kind of consciousness did ordinary individuals living their lives in China-Before-China, the vast majority of whom were peasants, have of the wider world? How did they conceive of their relationship with society, with the world beyond their village? Did they and could they feel connected to a larger community beyond the local? What filled and constituted their social imaginary? What role did illiteracy play in preventing the expansion of their imaginaries through culture?

For more than two millennia, the common culture of everyday life in China-Before-China was practised orally or with a very low level of literacy. As for oral culture, over the two final dynasties, the Ming and the Qing, it was 'compartmentalized and parochial', and 'while individuals who could read and write were to be found everywhere in China, in any particular region they formed only a small minority of the population.'[1] Indeed, communication across regions and between social classes was severely limited by widespread illiteracy and major linguistic diversity:

> Comparatively few people were able to read and comprehend everything in the literary tradition and a few more were able to read everything except the most difficult texts, and so on down

> through the degrees of difficulty or accessibility … In fact, the most meaningful subdivisions of the literate realm were related to class, as those of the oral realm were to geography.[2]

Any consciousness of belonging to a broader community other than the very local was severely hindered by the unavoidable limits of oral communication: 'there were two double barriers around the typical illiterate. He could not understand oral messages in dialects different than his own, or any written in a message; and he could not communicate with others if circumstances required either that he use another dialect, or the written word.'[3]

Cultural texts and practices were similarly limited for the vast illiterate majority of the Ming and Qing population. Even marketplace storytellers would have to rely on other passers of culture:

> An illiterate seventeenth century Nan-p'ing storyteller, for example, would have been steeped in Fukienese oral culture, but his knowledge of the oral culture of the Wu-speaking area to the north, or the Yueh-speaking region to the south, would have depended on that material having been translated into Min by bilingual intermediaries.[i] In the same way, his knowledge of the content of written texts could only have been indirect and mediated by one or more literate middlemen, who would certainly have introduced changes in the original text.[4]

Similarly, access to state-wide elite culture was severely restricted by the constraints of language and literacy, and again, what did filter down necessarily passed through middlemen:

i. In Nanp'ing or Nanping 南平, Fujian province, the local language was, and is, Min 閩, called Hoklo, Fúlǎo 福佬/Héluò 河洛 in Taiwan. Wu 吳 refers to the language spoken in the region now dominated by Shanghai; Yueh, or Yue 粵, refers to dialects of Cantonese.

> The illiterate could not transcend the world of folktales, sermons, legends, gossip, and hearsay—a rich and varied realm, but still confining. The teachings of the ritual scriptures, the adventures of the heroes of the Romance of the Three Kingdoms,[ii] the latest edict against heterodox religion, even a letter from home—all these had to be explained to him by someone who could read.[5]

As we have seen, at the end of the Qing dynasty—during the last decade of the nineteenth century and the first decade of the twentieth—the population of Qing territory stood at around 400 million, of which urban-dwellers accounted for around 6 per cent, or 24 million.[6] At the end of the Qing period, there was a 95 per cent illiteracy rate.[7] The statistics for women were far worse. In 1873 it was estimated that in Guangdong province, aside from 'nuns and actresses, taking city and country together … the average would be about one woman in a thousand who could read at all'; whilst in north China not one woman in 10,000 could read.[8]

At the end of the nineteenth century, only around 1 per cent of the overall population read newspapers or periodicals. This was despite the efforts of some progressive newspapers to make the literary language more accessible to a less literate readership.[9] Hoping to reach a wider audience, they employed what was called 'shallow literary language' (*qian wenli* 淺文理, or *qian wenyan* 淺文言), as opposed to the more sophisticated 'high literary language' (*shen wenli* 深文, literally 'deep' literary language, or simply *wenyanwen* 文言文). This 'lighter' version had been developed by nineteenth-century foreign missionaries and

ii. *The Romance of the Three Kingdoms* (*Sanguo yanyi* 三國演義) was a fictional historical romance set at the end of the Han and during the period of the Three Kingdoms or states (220–65 CE); it is attributed to the fourteenth-century author Luo Guanzhong 羅貫中.

translators of the Bible.[iii] However, it remained distant from the everyday vernacular, which would form the basis of the future National Language, and could do little to make the written word more accessible to the mass of illiterates.[10]

iii. In 1885 John Griffith (1831–1912) of the London Missionary Society (LMS) published his translation of the New Testament in *qian wenli*. See Yang Gefei 楊格非 [John Griffith], *Xinyue quanshu* 新約全書 [The Complete New Testament]. Griffith had established himself in the city of Hankow, now part of Wuhan, and altogether spent fifty years in China.

6

CHINESE LANGUAGE?

Behind me as I write is a wall of Chinese books; that is, books in the Chinese language and books mainly from China. By 'Chinese language' I mean the language that has been the written lingua franca of China for the past century. There is a chasm between that language and the written language of the elite culture that preceded it. To the untutored non-Chinese eye, it may all look like Chinese, but it is not.

To return to the books behind me, they all concern, or rather go to make up, what once would have been called 'modern Chinese literature'. However, I shall use the term 'Chinese literature of the twentieth century'. To talk of 'modern Chinese literature' is after all anachronistic, for 'Chinese' literature can only be modern. This was a literature written in a created vernacular language. It was, and remains, the literature of those Chinese who consider themselves 'Chinese' or rather members of the Han ethnicity; that is to say, the officially identified majority of those living within the borders of the Republic of China established in 1912, and subsequently of the People's Republic of China established in 1949, as well as those who fled to Taiwan in the same year. All the literature that went before is the literature of what we may call, once again, 'China-Before-China'.

The written language adopted some years after the 1911 Chinese Revolution, which toppled the Manchu dynasty, differs from what is now commonly, and once again anachronistically, known as 'classical Chinese'—a written language with a monosyllabic lexicon that stretches back at least 3,000 years. It has been described as:

> an ossified medium of written communication, largely divorced from its spoken sources, which apparently suited the increased needs for communication despite ever larger dialectal cleavages quite well. It was stabilized through the rise of bureaucracy, the canonization of texts, the consolidation of Confucianism as state doctrine, and, gradually, by new requirements in education. Despite the vernacular concussions provoked by the entry of Buddhism in the Eastern Han, and, much later, the contact with the West since the Ming period, it remained a formidably stable unified tool of communication.[1]

In talking about written Chinese, there is one important shibboleth that needs to be laid to rest. Often the visual aspect of the language leads the uninitiated to liken Chinese characters to hieroglyphs, or pictographs. The eminent French scholar of Chinese linguistics, Viviane Alleton, refutes this notion succinctly:

> Chinese characters are often presented to foreigners as little pictures, and there is no lack of teachers of Chinese who back up this fantasy. But if one shows a few characters to someone who has never learnt Chinese, characters either chosen at random or chosen for their supposed resemblances to what the character designates, it is immediately obvious the meaning remains a mystery. Supporters of the pictograph thesis will say that the difficulty stems from the evolution of the writing system and that originally when inscribed on tortoise shells, or bronzes, there were indeed images. Yet, someone with no knowledge of

> Chinese to whom one presented these shapes, reproduced exactly as on the originals, would no more be able to make them out than they would the contemporary characters.

She concludes that these archaic texts are in no way a series of images; rather, they consist of proper sentences, constituted from grammatical words, put together in a definite order.[2] However, as we shall see below, apart from the apparent visual similarity between the old dynastic language and today's Chinese, everything to do with grammar and word order distinguishes the two languages.

Pronunciation and Romanization

The Chinese language today uses characters to which phonetic values cannot be attributed by those who have not learned them. For the sake of foreigners needing at least to pronounce proper nouns, systems of transliteration were developed by Westerners. In the twentieth century Chinese authorities also adopted such systems, in order to facilitate the teaching of literacy. The official system that is most widespread today is *Hanyu pinyin*, literally 'Han language spell-sound'; it corresponds to the pronunciation of modern standard Chinese, or what Westerners commonly call Mandarin. The characters inherited from old language have been pronounced very differently over the millennia, and have also varied radically according to the region using them; but we need today to have sounds to refer to them. Thus, conventionally we have identified the pronunciation of 'Mandarin' with the characters used in *wenyanwen* 文言文, the 'ossified medium of communication', as I have just done in this sentence.

However, characters may be pronounced and read aloud differently in many dialects and languages, as they are in modern Cantonese and Japanese. For instance, the pronunciation of *wenyanwen* in today's standard Cantonese may be represented thus: *man jin man*. Convenience is the primary reason for transliterating the characters found in *wenyanwen* into Mandarin pronunciation—whether applying the current PRC pinyin system used in this book, or the old Anglo-American Wades-Giles system, or the French EFEO system. Yet doing so also serves to create a proximity between today's language of China and the language(s) used in the same territory over the past 2,000–3,000 years. This proximity is artificial, but it is an allusion that the PRC's authorities are happy to maintain. The use of an official *Putonghua* standard Chinese transliteration system helps the state recuperate past texts and culture for the present.

Over the past century, much research has gone into reconstructing the sound of the language as it evolved over the past two millennia or so. Among those providing a set of readings for the language of pre-Qin unification classics—that is, those texts from before before 221 BCE—foremost was Bernhard Karlgren, who established transliteration systems for what he termed 'Archaic Chinese' and 'Middle Chinese'.[3] Karlgren's reconstruction system was recently overhauled and revised by Baxter and Sagart, who use the term 'Old Chinese' to refer to the language of the classical texts in circulation in the first millennium BCE; their new approach has involved looking at dialects within the boundaries of today's China and at neighbouring languages.[4] While the modern standard Chinese pinyin transliteration of the characters of Confucius's name would be *Kongzi*, in the Baxter-Sagart system this would be rendered *[k]ʰˤoŋʔ *tsʔ and the name of the philosopher *Zhuangzi* would be *[ts]raŋ *tsʔ.

One final word on the 'ossified medium of communication': it is not necessary to know or speak Chinese in order to learn or translate this language. Indeed, competence in today's spoken or written Chinese only became a requirement in the training of Western sinologists in the 1960s–70s. Previously, many a respected sinologist or translator had been unable to hold a conversation in 'Mandarin'.

Written languages

The new written language not only differed from the old literary language; it differed too from the pre-twentieth-century written vernacular known as *baihua* 白話 ('plain speech'), which also has an extensive written narrative corpus. The current national language, barely 100 years old, is a largely polysyllabic one that has been developed with a grammar totally distinct from 'classical Chinese'. Instead it is based on the pre-existing vernacular, on regional varieties of spoken 'Chinese', and on the incorporation of thousands of Japanese translations of foreign, mainly English, words into characters or *Hanzi* 漢字, what the Japanese call *kanji*.[i] This language was known as *guoyu*

i. The origin and development of language employed in the spaces now known as China are much more complex than was once thought. 'Philosophical Chinese'—the language of such as Confucius and the 'Taoists' found in texts dating from before the Qin unification—has long been apprehended as significantly different from the standardized language practised from the Han onwards. However, recent research reveals a substantial number of distinctions from its successor(s). For instance, Wolfgang Behr tells us that the language in use before 'unification' by the Qin, 'the language reconstructable on the basis of the *Shijing* 詩經 rhyming patterns, of the phonophoric or *xiesheng* 諧聲 series implied by the writing system, of Middle Chinese distinctions retrievable from rhyme dictionaries and several other types of evidence, probably was a *very* different language from its post-Qin successors. And it certainly did not resemble *any* of the modern dialects.' (Behr's emphasis.) Moreover, what Behr calls the 'Old Chinese language' 'was non-tonal and had a fairly complex syllable structure, allowing for initial consonant clusters, and the presence of "iambic" (schwa-vocalized) minor syllables preceding the main syllable'. Behr, 'Role of Language in Early Chinese Constructions of Ethnic Identity', p. 568.

國語 or 'national language' during the first half of the twentieth century, as it still is on Taiwan today, and has been known in the People's Republic of China since 1949 as *Putonghua* 普通話, literally 'common language'.

After 1949, a succession of writing-system reforms changed the visual aspect of the language, so that we now talk of *zhengtizi* 正體字 or *fantizi* 繁體字 (full-form characters) on the one hand, and *jiantizi* 簡體字 ('simplified' characters) on the other. Full-form characters are used exclusively on Taiwan, in Hong Kong and in much of the diaspora, while simplified characters are used exclusively in the People's Republic of China and also in Singapore. Furthermore, whereas for two millennia the language was written vertically from top to bottom and right to left, with no punctuation marks, in the PRC it is now written and printed, as with Western languages, horizontally from left to right, and with punctuation similar to that employed in European languages.

To illustrate the nature of the standard written language before the twentieth century, and how it differs from that in use afterwards, here is a short passage from the historian Sima Qian's version of the story of the 'Orphan of Zhao', dating from the second century BCE (originally the text would have been laid out vertically):

1) Original in full-form characters, laid out horizontally left to right:

盾雖不知猶為賊首以臣弑君子孫在朝何以懲罪請誅之

2) Original in simplified characters, laid out horizontally left to right:

盾虽不知犹为贼首以臣弑君子孙在朝何以惩罪请诛之

3) Original with today's pinyin (Romanized) transliteration:

盾 雖 不 知 猶 為 賊 首 以 臣 弑 君 子 孫 在 朝 何 以 懲 罪 請 誅之:

dun sui bu zhi you wei zei shou yi chen shi jun zi sun zai chao he yi cheng zui qing zhu zhi

4) Original in today's Cantonese transliteration:

盾 雖 不 知 猶 為 賊 首 以 臣 弒 君 子 孫 在 朝 何 以 懲 罪 請 誅之

teon seoi bat zi jau wai caak sau ji san si gwan zi syun zoi ciu ho ji cing zeoi cing zyu zi

5) Translation into today's standard Chinese with pinyin transliteration:

赵盾虽然不知情, 但主犯还应该是他

Zhao Dun suiran bu zhiqing, dan zhufan hai yinggai shi ta.

臣子杀掉了君主, 他的子孙现在居然还在朝廷里做官

Chenzi shadiaole junzhu, ta de zisun xianzai juran haizai chaotingli zuo guan,

这样, 我们怎么来警戒其他犯罪的人呢？请大家同意我

zheyang, women zenme lai jingjie qita fanzui de ren ne? Qing dajia tongyi wo

的意见, 拿他们来问罪吧。

de yijian, na tamen lai wenzui ba.

6) English translation:

Even though Zhao Dun was not in the know, he was nevertheless the chief assassin. If a subject kills his lord and if his descendants serve at court, how are their crimes to be punished? Please have them executed.

Some twenty-three characters/syllables in the original unpunctuated text require seventy-six characters/syllables in the punctuated modern Chinese translation. In the language of the original, a single character/syllable corresponded to a word; in today's language many words are multisyllabic. Moreover the 'modern' grammar is totally different from the original syntax, and the punctuation now follows a Western model.

The other feature that often surprises the new learner coming to the language from any modern language is that in *wenyanwen*—the historical literary language whose characters are used today—there was no copula: no verb to express 'to be'. Thus there are verbless sentences consisting of a juxtaposition of nominal units. When teaching my students I sometimes use this formula: *X Y* 也. Here, 也, pronounced *ye* in modern standard Chinese, is a particle indicating that what precedes is a nominal sentence. Possible translations are:

X is Y
X is a case of Y
X is due to Y

as in:

宋小國也
Song xiao guo ye

宋/ 小國/ 也
Song/xiao guo/ye

X Y 也
Song is a small state.

Sometimes, only one noun or nominal unit precedes *ye*, which can thus be expressed *Y* 也:

馬也 *Ma ye*
Horse *ye* = It's a horse

天也 *Tian ye*
Heaven *ye* = It's because of Heaven

善人也 *shan ren ye*
Good person *ye* = S/he's a good person.

Compare this last sentence with the *Putonghua*, that is the standard Chinese, equivalent:

她/他是一個好人
Ta shi yi ge hao ren
S/he is a * good person = S/he is a good person.[ii]

This is a straightforward sentence with a verb meaning 'to be', which resembles much more closely the syntax of English than that of the *wenyanwen* of China-Before-China. There is only one character common to both sentences. That character is *ren* 人, meaning 'person'. The Latin equivalent would be *homo bonus est*; three words which in today's French would be *C'est un homme bon*.

For the purpose of clarifying the differences between the old and new languages, let us now examine two poetic texts. The first, *Luchai* 鹿柴 (Deer enclosure), is by the celebrated Tang poet Wang Wei 王維 (699–759 CE). It is composed in the written language of its day, and in a lyric form known as *wuyan jueju* 五言絕句, which has five monosyllabic words/characters for each sense unit or 'line', the entire poem consisting of four such 'lines' or verses. In pre-twentieth century editions, the poem is not laid out in lines or verses as such; readers simply knew that the end-stop occurred after every fifth character. Thus, in printed editions or in calligraphic scrolls hung up on walls, the five-character line was not

ii. Where * represents the classifier 個 *ge*; English too has classifiers such as 'crowd' as in a 'crowd of people', 'flock' in a 'flock of sheep'. *Ge* is the most common classifier in standard Chinese; Cantonese has a much greater panoply of such words.

necessarily respected. Below is the poem presented as a single line:

空
山
不
見
人
但
聞
人
響
返
景
入
深
林
復
照
青
苔
上

In modern, twentieth-century editions, we find punctuation dividing the poem into 'lines' of five syllables/characters, as in the 1976 Taiwan published edition of the classic anthology *Tangshi sanbai shou* 唐詩三百首 (Three Hundred Tang Poems):[5]

空
山
不
見
人
，
但

聞人語響。返景入深林，復照青苔上。

Nowadays, it is also customary in the People's Republic of China to set out the poem horizontally, in stanza form, and with punctuation, as if it were a modern Western-language poem:

鹿柴
空山不見人,
但聞人語響。,
返景入深林,
復照青苔上。,

Let us now try to make sense of the poem.[6] First, here it is with a modern pinyin transliteration. Again, each character corresponds to a single syllable, and each syllable/character is a word:

空	山	不	見	人
kong	*shan*	*bu*	*jian*	*ren*

但	聞	人	語	響
dan	*wen*	*ren*	*yu*	*xiang*
返	景	入	深	林
fan	*jing*	*ru*	*shen*	*lin*
復	照	青	苔	上
fu	*zhao*	*qing*	*tai*	*shang*

And here it is with a literal translation:

空	山	不	見	人
kong	*shan*	*bu*	*jian*	*ren*
empty	mountain	not	see	people
但	聞	人	語	響
dan	*wen*	*ren*	*yu*	*xiang*
only	hear	people	talk	sound
返	景	入	深	林
fan	*jing*	*ru*	*shen*	*lin*
return	light	enter	deep	forest
復	照	青	苔	上
fu	*zhao*	*qing*	*tai*	*shang*
again	shine	green	lichen	on.

Here is my translation:

An empty mountain seeing no-one
But hearing the sound of people talking
Reflected light enters the deep forest
Once more shining on the green moss

Here is Robinson's from the Penguin *Wang Wei*:

Hills empty, no-one to be seen
We only hear voices echoed—

With light coming back into the deep wood
The top of the green moss is lit again[7]

Here is Burton Watson's rendering:

Empty hills, no-one in sight,
Only the sound of someone talking:
Late sunlight enters the deep wood,
Shining over the green moss again.[8]

The syntax of the language in which this poem is composed is radically different from that of today's Chinese, and the old poetic language itself often represented a departure from prose syntax. Here, as Watson has remarked, the poem, 'superficially couched in the plainest language, exploits the economy and vagueness of [the language] to suggest a wealth of philosophical subtleties lurking beneath the surface.'[9] There were also rules of rhyme and metre to respect which are impossible to reproduce in translation.

One important feature of the literary language under the dynasties of China-Before-China is that words often had multiple grammatical functions, thus a word could be a noun, a verb, or another part of speech, depending on word order and context; compare with the word 'impact', which in modern English may be a verb or a noun depending on the context. In the poem above, as Watson points out, the word *shang* 上 could be either a positional word (translatable as 'on', 'on top of', 'over'), or a full verb (translatable as 'ascend' or 'rise'). The second interpretation alters the sense of the final line, to 'a picture of sunlight retreating up the side of the mountain as the sun drops behind an obscuring peak.'[10] Similarly, questions of tense, number and declension do not arise in *wenyanwen* 文言文, thus giving a greater flexibility—but also greater responsibility—to the reader/translator.

The original allows all of the above translations, but what I have attempted to show is how much more constrained the translator is by a poem in today's *Putonghua*, a language whose syntax resembles English more closely than it does the literary language of China-Before-China. After the ravages of the Cultural Revolution (1966–76), writers attempted to recreate a literary language. Nevertheless, compared to the rather unstable new poetic language of the 1920s, the idiom available to poets in the 1970s was a fixed national language out of which, as with any modern national language, the author could—with wit, imagination, and creativity—craft a text that respected the function of poetry, as standing out from, and against, everyday speech.

Below is a poem written in 1982 in contemporary Chinese by the poet Duo Duo 多多 (1951–), who like many others wrote clandestinely during the Cultural Revolution, and whose style is associated with a 'school' known as 'Misty poetry' (*menglongshi* 朦朧詩), which bears comparison with Western surrealism or Imagism. Here is my translation:

THE BIG ROCK WE CANNOT CLIMB

That's the big rock we cannot climb
To make it
We debated six years
We made it then climbed upwards
You said it probably needed seven years more
Probably another eight
Or a longer time
Time enough for an appendicitis
The operation took ten years
It was just like the flash of a knife—[11]

Here is the text in the original:

那是我们不能攀登的大石

那是我们不能攀登的大石
为了造出他
我们议论了六年
我们造出它又向上攀登
你说大约还有七年
大约还要八年
一个更长的时间
还来得及一次阑尾炎
手术进行了十年
好像刀光
一闪——[12]

Here is the poem transliterated and with a word-for-word translation:

那	是	我们	不	能	攀登	的	大	石
na	*shi*	*women*	*bu*	*neng*	*pandeng*	*de*	*da*	*shi*
That	is	we	not	can	climb	[…]	big	rock

为了	造出	它
weile	*zaochu*	*ta*
In order	to create	it

我们	议论	了	六	年
Women	*yilun*	*le*[iii]	*liu*	*nian*
we	debate-	-d	six	years

我们	造出	它	又	向上	攀登
women	*zaochu*	*ta*	*you*	*xiangshang*	*pandeng*
we	create	it	then	upwards	climb

iii. *le* 了 = past tense indicator.

你	说	大约	还	要	七	年
Ni	*shuo*	*dayue*	*hai*	*yao*	*qi*	*nian*
you (sing.)	say	probably	still	need	seven	years

大约	还	要	八	年
dayue	*hai*	*yao*	*ba*	*nian*
probably	still	need	eight	years

一	个	更	长	的	时间
Yi	*ge*[iv]	*geng*	*chang*	*de*	*shijian*
a/one	[…]	even more	long	[…]	time

还	来得及	一	次	阑尾炎
hai	laideji	yi	ci	lanweiyan
still	time enough	one	time	appendicitis

手术	进行	了	十	年
shouxu	*jinxing*	*le*	*shi*	*nian*
operation	execute-	d	ten	years

好像	刀	光
haoxiang	*dao*	*guang*
like	knife	light

一	闪 ——
yi	*shan*
a/one	flash.

The lines of the poem are of irregular length, and, as can be seen from the transliteration, words may be monosyllabic or multisyllabic. As is the case with much modernist poetry anywhere in the twentieth century, the poet uses no punctuation. There is no rhyme scheme, but six of the lines end with the

iv. Chinese nouns are often preceded by a 'measure word' or classifier, for example: *yi qun niao*—群鳥 'one flock [of] birds'; *ge* 个/個 is the most common measure word, here used to qualify 'time': a period of time, a spell of time.

sound *-ian*, which occurs four times in the word for 'year', *nian* 年. There is no regular metre; the poem is written, as was the vast majority of twentieth-century poetry, in free verse.[v] In modernist poetry, lines may be run-on or, as here, line-stopped; the lack of punctuation often creates ambiguity which is another feature of such poetry. The syntax of modern standard Chinese is quite similar to English. However, nouns are qualified by placing the qualifying phrase plus the particle *de* 的 in front of them (line 1: 'na shi women bu neng pandeng *de* da shi'—'That is we cannot climb [...] big rock' = 'That is the big rock we cannot climb'). Past tense, or a change in circumstances, is indicated by placing the particle *le* 了 after the verb. The vocabulary is straightforward, plain even, but is here used poetically, creatively.

The clear syntax and simple vocabulary mean that, unlike the poem by Wang Wei, there is limited room for flexibility in translation. Nevertheless, Duo Duo's poem is not easy to understand, and interpretation will depend on other factors such as context and the reader's knowledge of Chinese history and society. We cannot be in the mind of the poet; we cannot know his intention. But we can have an idea of how readers in 1982 might have read the poem. Its theme of counting years is important. An urban reader over the age of twenty in 1982 would recognize the numbers. 'Ten years' was

v. The principal model for Chinese New Poetry (*Xinshi* 新詩), when it was first written in the 1920s and 1930s, was French *vers libre* or free verse. A few anglophile poets, such as Wen Yiduo 聞一多 (1899–1946), experimented with introducing a new metrics based on the feet of English-language poetry, but this initiative failed to gain favour. The shackles of old poetry having just been shaken off, most young poets craved the freedom *vers libre* offered. Wen Yiduo, because he adopted regular line length, was known as the 'tofu poet' (*doufu shiren* 豆腐詩人) since the layout of his poems reminded readers of rectangular trays of uniformly cut tofu.

officially the length of the Cultural Revolution that stretched from 1966 to the death of Mao and the fall of the Gang of Four in 1976. The poem can be read in such a light. But then, perhaps there is a more personal 'we', a 'we' pertaining to a couple, to a group. This is a modernist, Imagistic poem; it is precisely this quality of unknowability, of indeterminability, that enraged the authorities, who declared such poetry 'obscure' (*menglong* 朦朧); a quality shared with modernist poetry elsewhere and also with much of the poetry of the elite in premodern China-Before-China.

Over 1,200 years separate the two poems. Duo Duo writes in a modern language, one whose first tentative literary creations stretch back no further than the 1920s. Wang Wei wrote in a language that already had more than a thousand years of literary history behind it. No present-day reader of today's Chinese language could make much sense of poetry such as Wang Wei's without being trained to do so—just as no normally educated Anglophone reader could make sense of *Beowulf*, a Greek access Homer, or an Italian understand Virgil[vi] Once again, to the untrained Western eye it all may look like Chinese, but is not.

Beyond what might be read by our modern eyes as a 'transcendent' common poetic sentiment, this exercise has demonstrated the immense difference between the dynastic literary written language, used by the elite for over 2,000 years, and

vi. Elite bilingual competence in *wenyanwen*, the language of the premodern era, and the new national language *guoyu* 國語, was a temporary and historically specific phenomenon that concerned only the poets and novelists of the 1920s–1940s who had in their youth been trained in 'traditional' schools. The poets and writers of Duo Duo's generation, born after the founding of the People's Republic of China in 1949, were schooled in the 1950s and 1960s and received a modern, not to say revolutionary, education.

today's language. It also partly shows the proximity of modern Chinese to English, when the Chinese characters are stripped away. Today's language is both the repository and the vehicle of its users' expectations and imaginaries; it both created and was created by the modern polity called China. But how was this language made?

7

THE MAKING OF A NATIONAL LANGUAGE

At the beginning of the twentieth century there had already been calls for a 'national language', in other words a national vernacular language. As early as 1906, in one of the first recorded appeals for the use of *guoyu* 國語, a group of returned students from Japan had demanded a programme to 'train people to speak the national language in order to eliminate the dialects of the provinces'.[1] But when the fledgling Republic of China was established in 1912, there was no official provision for any such new, national language.[2] A committee for the standardization of pronunciation, established by the Ministry of Education in 1912, proposed a set of thirty-nine phonetic symbols (*zhuyin fuhao* 注音符號); but it was not until November 1918 that it was adopted as a 'phonetic alphabet', for a time the symbols even being promoted as an alternative to characters. This system of pronunciation, or transliteration, later called *laoguoyin* 老國音 (Old National Pronunciation), was largely based on Beijing Mandarin, but included other features. The system was revised in 1932, and *xinguoyin* 新國音 (New National Pronunciation) became totally based on Beijing Mandarin.[3]

One of the major problems faced by translators was how to render foreign names and concepts in characters. Either they could attempt to represent the sounds of foreign words, or they could translate the sense. In the first half of the twentieth century, there were hundreds of foreign words that were simply transliterated, names of countries for instance. 'France' was transliterated as 法蘭西 (literally 'law-orchid-west'); when pronounced in Mandarin, this sounds like *fa-lan-syee* (written *falanxi* in the current pinyin system), while in Cantonese it is pronounced *fa-lan-say*. Indeed, many of the early transliterations passed through Cantonese. Even today, the reason behind the transliteration of some countries' names seems obscure and puzzling until pronounced in Cantonese. Sweden is represented by the characters 瑞典 (literally 'auspicious-statute'), pronounced 'ray-dee-en' or *ruidian* in Mandarin; in Cantonese the characters are pronounced 'soy-din'. The Cantonese attempt to reproduce the English 'Sweden' came first, and Mandarin speakers later simply pronounced what was written down.

Concepts were similarly transliterated. During the first half of the twentieth century, the word for 'modern'—in the sense of contemporary, up-to-date—was rendered 摩登, 'mor-dung' or *modeng* in today's pinyin. For decades, the process of modernization was simply referred to as 'Westernization'; later the concept would be translated as 現代 *xiandai* ('present-period'). Numerous words passed into Chinese through modern Japanese, whose linguists had used Chinese characters, or *kanji* in Japanese, to invent new words for Western concepts.[4] For names, Liang Qichao at the end of the nineteenth century had recommended 'using the English pronunciation as the norm for representing all sounds in Occidental languages, while Beijing dialect [Mandarin] … could be used for translating foreign names.'[5]

Nevertheless, many words in today's Chinese still illustrate their Cantonese heritage; the word for ice-cream is half-translated, half-transliterated as 冰淇淋, pronounced 'bing-chee-lin' (*bingqilin*) in Mandarin, in which 冰 *bing* means 'ice' and 淇淋 is pronounced 'kay-lam' in Cantonese, a transliteration of the

English 'cream'. Of course, in Mandarin transliteration the etymology of the word is lost. All of which illustrates the unplanned, haphazard and diverse evolution of a modern idiom, striving to accommodate local linguistic differences and to absorb foreign names and concepts, even before a nation or a national language had come into being.

Right up until the 1920s, there was no formal written language with which to replace the 'officialese', the written lingua franca that was *wenyanwen*—the language of China-Before-China's daily paperwork, of the elite literati and their literature. While *wenyanwen* had been co-extensive with the territory ruled by the dynastic sovereigns, it was no national language, since the vast majority could not read or write it. There existed colloquial or vernacular texts, but these represented language that had been mainly used for story-telling and could not accommodate the demands of a modern state. And yes, there was the spoken lingua franca, which facilitated communication between officials (mandarins) regardless of where they hailed from.[6] However, what did not exist was a territory-wide, commonly understood, written and spoken language such as had been developed and taught in France or Germany by the end of the nineteenth century.[i] After all, at the end of the nineteenth century, in what was still the territory of the Manchu Dynasty *Da Qing guo* 大清國 ('Great Qing state'), there was no

i. At the time of the French Revolution (1789), '50% of Frenchmen did not speak [French] at all, only 12–13% spoke it "correctly"' and in 'northern and southern France virtually nobody talked French' (Hobsbawm, *Nations and Nationalism*, pp. 60–1). But the proclamation of the French Republic would radically alter the status and spread of French, from a king's language merely encouraged among his subjects to a national language that it was the duty of republican citizens to employ. See Hobsbawm, *Nations and Nationalism*, pp. 101–30; and Thiesse, *La Création des identités nationales*, p. 70.

nation-state, only a wished-for nation; and since illiteracy was the norm, there was not only no 'national' language, but no language at all with which to unite the common people.

The Qing had no interest in uniting the common people, for whom in any case language was not a primary concern.[ii] It was the commitment and insistence of young intellectuals in the publishing and educational spheres that led to the concretization of demands for the institution of a national language. In September 1915, the soon-to-be Communist Party leader, Chen Duxiu 陳獨秀 (1879–1942), launched 青年雜誌 *Qingnian zazhi* (*Youth* magazine), which a year later became 新青年 *Xin qingnian* (*New Youth*). From the beginning, the magazine also sported a French title, *La Jeunesse*.[7] It was written entirely in the vernacular, or in what would come to be called the 'national language'.[iii]

ii. 'For the illiterate among the common people the world of words was entirely oral, and consequentially the language of official or any other writing was of no significance except, increasingly, as a reminder of their lack of knowledge and power.' Hobsbawm, *Nations and Nationalism*, pp. 114–15.

iii. The French title *La Jeunesse* foregrounded the desire of its editors to show the modernity, the Westernness, of their project. France and the use of the French language signified aspiration to a liberty that English, the language of China's then main enemy, the British, could not provide. Later on, in 1932, the popular literary journal *Xiandai* 現代, literally 'modern'/'modern times', would adopt the French co-title *Les Contemporains* (The Contemporaries). It is worth noting that the characters on the cover (see Fig. 3) are to be read from right to left, not from left to right as is the case in European languages and in present-day Chinese publications. Similarly, the insert showing the contents should be read from top to bottom. By the 1970s, it was the English language, associated with the world beyond, with open society and freedom, that attracted young writers and intellectuals; the cover of the now renowned literary magazine established by the poet Bei Dao 北岛, *Jintian* 今天, was emblazoned with the English-language co-title *TODAY!*

Nevertheless, it was not until the 1920s that the existing written vernacular and spoken Mandarin were adopted as the basis for a new national language of the new nation-state called China. In January 1920, the Ministry of Education decided that the vernacular would be used in the first two years of primary education, and its adoption quickly spread to higher echelons of the school system. In 1920–1, the northern vernacular was officially recognized as the 'national language' or *guoyu* 國語.[8]

The campaign for a national language based on the already existing written vernacular and on the spoken northern dialect ('Mandarin') was led by the 4 May Movement students, literary journalists, and educators. Although the literary use of modern written language based on the spoken vernacular had been suggested for some time by such cultural luminaries as Liang Qichao and Huang Zunxian 黃遵憲 (1848–1905), and notwithstanding early efforts by the dominant literary figure of the time, Lu Xun 魯迅 (1881–1936), the prime movers of the national language were Hu Shi (1891–1962) 胡適 and *La Jeunesse* founder Chen Duxiu. It was Hu who first insisted on the interconnection of new literary creation and a new national language. In a 1918 piece entitled *Guoyu de wenxue-wenxue de guoyu* 國語的文學—文學的國語 ('National Language Literature: A Literary National Language'), he writes in model vernacular Chinese:

> Once we have 'real literature' and 'living literature', 'false literature' and 'dead literature' will disappear by themselves.
>
> ... The literary revolution we have advocated simply aims to create a national-language literature for China. Only when we have a national-language literature will we have a literary national language. Only once we have a literary national language can our national language be counted as a genuine

national language. If national language has no literature, then it has no life, has no value, cannot establish itself, cannot be developed.[9]

The French sociologist Pierre Bourdieu stresses the central importance of writing to the genesis of the state, referring to the 'unification of the linguistic market, this unification of the market of writing which is coextensive with the state':

[I]t is the state that makes it [writing] while making itself. One of the ways in which the state makes itself is to standardize spelling, to standardize weights and measures, to standardize the law … the school system is also a process through which we standardize individuals who are homogenized in terms of writing, spelling, and the way they speak.[10]

Such was also the ambition of the builders of the Chinese nation-state.

The national language in the Republic of China had to be accessible to the common people, the vast majority of whom were not literate—literally in Chinese did not 'recognize characters'—and who entertained themselves through songs, stories and performances passed down orally in local languages and 'dialects'. Indeed, Hu Shi recognized the need for incorporating such language into the new official vernacular; he was among the first to use the term 'dialect literature' (*fangyan de wenxue* 方言的文學): 'Since the vernacular language … is often expressed in a colloquial manner, and the colloquial language is in turn often expressed in local dialect form, it goes without saying that there is an intrinsic link between the national language and dialects.'[11] The national language was to replace an elite language that had first diverged from colloquial language 2,000 years previously—if indeed the written language ever corresponded to a single spoken language, and if the written language had ever been comprehensively commensurate with it. As to the existing, premodern written vernacular, it was deemed insufficient and inadequate for articulating and expressing a new nation-state avid for science, technology and modern economics—in other words, capitalist modernity.

As we have seen, 'the conventional story of the emergence of China as a modern nation-state is … fundamentally flawed because it takes for granted that "Chinese people" are *inherently* a nation and that "China" is *inherently* a nation-state.'[12] In other words, before the twentieth century there was no Chinese nation-state, no Chinese nation and no China as such. Indeed, '"China" as a country and a project, is arguably but one hundred years old.'[13] Previously, there had simply been a succession of more or less centrally ruled states governed by a series of dynasties. These were, for much of the past 2,000 years, states comprised of territories in which dozens of distinct languages, and even more dialects, were spoken. These were territories whose customs, foodstuffs, eating habits, housing and clothing were substantially varied, the whole space being unified, like the Ottoman and Habsburg Empires, by an overarching state-bureaucratic machine with its own elite language and culture.

This explains in part the ideological acrobatics involved in describing and explaining the People's Republic of China. When we strip away the rhetoric of Communism—now a mere warped parody of the Marxism-Leninism that nevertheless remains the state's official credo—the essential task of China's rulers over the past century has been to advance and to consolidate the construction of a Chinese nation-state. But within the borders of that 'nation-state' live numerous, officially fifty-five, ethnic minorities, the best-known being the Tibetans and the Uighurs. Each minority attempts to use its own language, where one survives, and to practise its own customs and religion. As for those officially designated part of the

'Han' Chinese ethnicity, the notional majority, while many speak some variety of modern standard Chinese, or what in the West we persist in calling Mandarin, many also speak other languages, such as Cantonese, Wu (the language of the Shanghai region), and Hoklo/Minnanhua, the language of Fujan and Taiwan.[14]

While internally lip-service may be paid to the Chinese state's multi-ethnic, multi-lingual nature, externally official discourse rarely parades this diversity. Chinese people, as understood by foreigners, are quite simply those people who look like Chinese; who look like the officials shown on the evening news, or who resemble the person behind the counter in the local Chinese takeaway.[iv] To the foreigner, and outside of China, the diversity and divergence contained within the borders of the PRC and its diaspora are quite simply hidden behind a mask of seeming 'Chineseness'.

***

To return to the books shelved behind me, they represent the literary production of the only polity or cultural entity that has ever called itself *China* or *Zhongguo* 中國, and one that is resolutely modern. They are a monument to a more or less successful twentieth-century national(izing) linguistic and literary project. Along another wall of my study, to my left, are shelves of books containing the literature and the knowledge of a time before this China. But most of the books printed and published in the twentieth and twenty-first centuries, whether written in Chinese, English or French, nevertheless identify themselves

iv. The post-9/11 anti-Islamic global 'war on terror' gave the authorities the excuse to clamp down on Islamic minorities, and propagation of the idea of China as a multi-ethnic state has waned; the authorities have reinforced Han Chinese control of all ethnic regions—in the case of Xinjiang, in a particularly brutal manner.

with 'China' or 'Chinese'. In the case of books dealing with poetry and other literary genres, they specify that they concern the 'old', 'ancient', or 'classical', *gu* 古 in Chinese. However, both these terms, 'Chinese' and *gu*, are anachronistic. For instance, before the twentieth century, poetry was simply poetry (*shi* 詩)—not 'classical' poetry (*gushi* 古詩).[15]

As we have seen, Europeans have been identifying the space and its dominant official language and literary culture as 'China'/'Chinese' since the sixteenth century, and so when Arthur Waley (1889–1966) entitled his selection of old poetry *Chinese Poems*, there was a certain Orientalist sense to it. However the poems he translates are all from before the twentieth century and are not written in today's Chinese. Thus 'Chinese' here refers only to the poetry of China-Before-China, and excludes the poetry of China the nation-state.[16] The twentieth-century French sinologist Paul Demiéville, on the other hand, chose *Anthologie de la poésie chinoise classique* (Anthology of Classical Chinese Poetry); a title explicitly acknowledging that the poetry he translated dated from another, earlier era, and thus leaving open the possible existence of another poetry—one in a different, later language, that of the twentieth century.[17]

Further along the bookshelf is a bilingual anthology produced in the People's Republic of China and quite clearly aimed at the foreign reader—*Gems of Chinese Poetry: Zhongguo shige jinghua* 中國詩歌精华—in whose title there is no mention of 'classical', 'ancient' or *gu* 古. On examining the contents the reasoning is clear: the ambition of this slender volume is to blur the difference between lyric creation before and after the beginning of the twentieth century, spanning 2,500 years. It goes from the *Shijing* 詩經 or *Book of Songs*, dating from the eleventh to seventh centuries BCE, up to the verse of Ai Qing 艾青, father of the celebrated contemporary artist Ai Weiwei 艾未未.[18]

Poetry written in a language that is not the current, national language has thus been recuperated to the modern nationalizing project. Premodern poetry, the poetry of the China-Before-China, becomes the poetry of *Zhongguo* 中國.

Yet, as we saw in the comparison between the Tang dynasty Wang Wei and the contemporary Duo Duo, these two poetries are composed in two different languages, more different than Latin is from modern French. Once again we find two distinct literatures in two distinct languages, seamlessly conflated into one lyric continuum. This is to do a great injustice to the ambitions and achievements of China's modern poets, who were deliberately iconoclastic, eschewed premodern versification, and modelled their poetry on Western, almost exclusively French and English, poetry. Between the poetry of the twentieth century and the poetry written according to the rules of premodern versification—in a language as distant from today's Chinese as Greek is from English—there exists a chasm of incomprehensibility. Chinese poetry is more akin to the French or English lyric tradition than to the poetic tradition in what is now China. Every sinologist knows this, but the uninitiated eye that can distinguish at a glance between 'contemporary' Chinese art and premodern paintings is blind to the difference of the written word.[v]

To sum up, the architects of China the nation-state have renamed and reclassified knowledge, language and creative

v. Sinologists schooled in premodern poetry may be quite dismissive of modern and contemporary poetry. Sometimes that may simply be because they do not find it very good by its own lights, but often it is because they find modern poetry compares poorly with the old poetry they appreciate. In the 1990s there was a major academic controversy about the 'value' of contemporary Chinese poetry. See Owen, 'What is World Poetry?', pp. 28–32; and see my discussion and refutation of this article in Lee, *Troubadours, Trumpeters, Troubled Makers*, pp. 93–101.

practices as either 'Chinese' or 'ancient' or 'traditional' when, for thousands of years, these were simply knowledge, writing, or painting.

The recent work by Craig Clunas goes a long way towards explaining the genesis of the Western, and consequently the current Chinese, understanding of 'traditional', 'Chinese' painting.[19] It was largely constructed by Japanese art scholars in the early twentieth century, and resulted in a narrow and premodern signification being attached to art produced in (the space we now call) China, thus leaving Japan as the privileged source of modern Asian art.[20] As Clunas puts it, 'if Chinese painting had a history, it had, as seen from London in 1910, no present and hence no future. It was circumscribed, catalogued, known.'[21] Thus the term 'Chinese painting' designated a moment before the creation of both China the nation-state, and the very practices of 'Chinese painting', a painting of China. It is therefore paradoxical that the term used in Chinese today to refer to old conventional painting should be *guohua* 國畫 ('national painting'), whereas contemporary painting in China today is not seen as national, but is termed rather *Zhongguo dangdai yishu* 中国当代艺术, literally 'China contemporary art'.[22] Once again, when it came to division of knowledge and culture, the indebtedness of the emerging Chinese nation-state to foreign conceptual frameworks is revealed by the loan-words adopted to describe and contain both the old and the new.

The word for 'fine art' *meishu* 美術 is a prime example. Its appearance in Chinese may be represented schematically thus:

beaux arts → *schöne Kunst* → *bijutsu* 美術 → *meishu* 美術

Here the Japanese translates the French/German *beaux/schöne* as *bi* 美 (literally 'beauty'), and *arts/Kunst* as *jutsu* 術 ('art'). The word *bijutsu* 美術 was then borrowed in China and pronounced in Chinese as *meishu*.[23] Once again, because the components of the imported Japanese word are written in *kanji* 漢字, literally 'Han characters', the Japanese origins of the neologism *meishu* are easily masked, as were those of thousands of other Japanese words that entered the Chinese language at the time.[vi] Once again, it all looks Chinese, even when it is 'Japanese'.

Another example of the obfuscation caused by the loose use of the term 'Chinese' concerns the medicine that was practised before the modern period, now reinvented as Traditional Chinese Medicine (TCM) or, in China, simply *Zhongyi* 中醫 ('Chinese medicine')—in opposition to *Xiyi* 西醫 or 'Western medicine'. Before the twentieth century, there was no 'Chinese medicine', there was just medicine; or rather there was a raft of practices that were called medicine, each ethnicity and region also enjoying its own medicines and practices. Recent studies have sought to demonstrate how TCM is the product of a modern process of recuperation, invention and reinvention. For instance, Bridie Andrews's *Making of Modern Chinese Medicine* has shown 'how traditional practices came to be called Chinese medicine', suggesting 'the fabric of modern Chinese medicine was woven with available threads from missionary, European, and Japanese medical models.'[24/25]

For many sinologists and China specialists—I should say for most of them—the early twentieth-century rupture with the preceding culture was no more than a hiatus in a long tradition of cultural production, leaving intact the status of

vi. Characters (kanji or Hanzi 漢字) imported into Japan over a period of centuries formed one of the scripts in which written Japanese developed, with both *hiragana* and *katakana* developing out of *kanji*. Whilst *wenyanwen* was used in the first instance at court, during the ninth to twelfth centuries CE it was adapted so as to be read with local pronunciation and to accord with local grammar; this adapted language was known as *kanbun*.

the older culture as the fountain and foundation of 'Modern' China. Dominant Sinology simply sees postdynastic creativity as an insipid tail-end, a poor orphaned child of what went before. However, here we can draw a parallel between creativity in modern Europe and its relationship to past 'civilization'. Cornelius Castoriadis, discussing the relationship of European culture and premodern creative practice with Paul Ricoeur, countered the French philosopher's assertion that '*la nouveauté absolue est impensable*' (total novelty is unthinkable), by positing a new kind of society and culture which could, indeed must, be instituted and created, and not simply reconfigured, reproduced, or recombined from pre-existent elements: 'While staying in the realm of Greco-occidental or European history … which begins with Homer, all sense, each new form that emerges is not the result of a combination of pre-existing forms, even if it maintains a certain referential link to that past.'[vii]

Castoriadis's idea of the novelty of forms, while itself anchored in yet another imagined continuity of 'Greco-occidental or European history', is transposable to China, the nation-state and republic created in 1912. While there were and are numerous lingering references to the past, the ambition was to create a new language, culture and ideology. In the case of twentieth-century China, these references to the past are also frequently displaced spatially onto the history of the West. The West's past may represent for the Chinese creator a

vii. Castoriadis would probably not have perceived such a parallel between China and Europe; while he remains an important theorist of the collective imaginary (in other words the way we, often falsely, imagine our world), he was sometimes, like many European academics, blinkered to Asian realities, falling back on inherited Western stereotypes when considering the rest of the world. See Marker, 'Interview with Cornelius Castoriadis', from 1989.

source of novelty as interesting and as recoverable as the West's present. To take again the example of Chinese twentieth-century poetry, this art form exhibits a total rupture with the language and form of the so-called 'tradition', yet its references to and borrowings from the past frequently concern the modern Euro-American 'tradition'.

This is not to underestimate the remnants of practices pertaining to China-Before-China that clung to the fabric of what was becoming the new nation-state; these survived in the ways that many Chinese imagined and lived their everyday lives. Even today there persists a multitude of artistic, linguistic and performative popular practices and customs that existed in their diverse forms within the borders of China-Before-China.[viii]

Writing of social and political change in medieval Europe, Castoriadis says, 'creation always takes place *in* the already there and, also, *through* the means offered by the already there. That does not prevent it from being formal creation'.[26] In other words, the novelty of creation is not impaired by its relation to another time or space, whilst being *new* it is always contingent. Indeed, the absence of a 'China-wide' common culture would in the twentieth century necessitate an aggressive, agglomerative reinventing of existing local popular cultures, and the 'creation' of new, national cultures, both popular and elite—a strategy common to the nation-building projects of both left- and right-wing nationalists.

There were, however, twentieth-century culturally conservative elements that clung to the past, to the cultural practices and forms that were predominantly the preserve of the literati-bureaucrat, state-wide elite in dynastic 'China'. Even amongst the Communist elite there was an ingrained, and somewhat

viii. As we shall see later in the discussion of local oral performance traditions.

contradictory and hypocritical, conservatism; a tendency that survives to this day. In the 1930s and 1940s, while the party advocated revolutionary national literature, Mao Zedong and Zhou Enlai both composed poems in premodern forms, even though the content often related to contemporary guerrilla campaigns or military action.

Mao used a particular form of poetry named *ci* 詞, literally 'words/lyrics'. *Ci* were originally song lyrics; every song or poem is identified with a melody or tune pattern (*cipai* 詞牌). More than 800 tune patterns are known. However, all the tunes themselves are lost. What remains is the versification, the technical restraints: the tone pattern, line lengths, and rhymes specific to each tune. Later *ci* poems using a particular *cipai* do not borrow the lyrics themselves, but nevertheless allude to the pre-existing poems, with the tune pattern providing an indirect aural reference to the original poem. Lyricists reused an original melody over and over, putting their own words to it. The new songs were sometimes, but far from always, distinguished by an additional title, a *ciming* 詞名 ('lyric title'). For example, Mao composed two *ci* poems with the tune pattern *Qin Yuan Chun* 沁园春, which was famously used by the outstanding Song dynasty poet, essayist, painter and statesman Su Shi 蘇軾 (1037–1102), also known as Su Dongpo 蘇東坡. Mao added the lyric titles 'Changsha' 長沙 (1925) and 'Snow' *Xue* 雪 (1936).

Su Dongpo's poem, written in 1074, bids farewell to his brother, who has been assigned to a distant administrative post. Here, in the second part of the poem, he recalls the happy times the two had spent studying together in the capital:

> When we lodged together in Chang'an, like the youthful Lu brothers just arrived,
> Our brushes dashed off a thousand words, we soaked up a thousand books,

Advising kings like Yao and Shun would present no challenge.
Time alone dictates if we are used or discarded, yet to advance or not is for us to decide,
Why not wait and see hands in sleeves, with hale and sturdy bodies,
We may go through life carefree, playing games over goblets of wine.[27/ix]

Mao's use of the same tune pattern in his 1925 poem, about his student days, would inevitably echo in the ears of the educated reader, evoking the poetic sentiment of Su Dongpo's much earlier work. Mao sets a more aggressive tone as the narrator departs Changsha, the provincial capital of Hunan, for new adventures:

I was here with a throng of companions,
Vivid yet those crowded months and years.
Young we were, schoolmates,
At life's full flowering;
Filled with student enthusiasm
Boldly we cast all restraints aside.
Pointing to our mountains and rivers,
Setting people afire with our words,
We counted the mighty no more than muck.
Remember still
How, venturing midstream, we struck the waters
And waves stayed the speeding boats?[28]

Mao Zedong was a member of neither the literati class nor the new intellectual elite, and was unenthusiastic about new

ix. Chang'an 長安 served as the capital to more than ten dynasties. The Lu brothers were young literari who stayed together in the Western Jin (265–316) capital, Luoyang. Yao 姚 and Shun 舜 were two legendary wise monarchs said to have lived towards the end of the third millennium BCE.

Western-style literary forms.[x] His main cultural baggage consisted of readings of fourteenth- to eighteenth-century vernacular fiction. In this Mao was in the company of other twentieth-century Chinese of a similar social background—rich peasant or provincial petit bourgeoisie—who continued to consume a literature written in a more accessible, if outdated, vernacular. This narrative in China-Before-China had grown out of historiography; as Cyril Birch has remarked, in 'the earliest historical writings we find the structured dialogues that would later constitute a staple resource for fiction.'[29] In later centuries, prior to the Sui 隋 reunification in 589 CE, 'Tales of marvels and demons, ghosts and reincarnations, set up new dimensions for the interpretation of mortal experience … By the Tang period two developments of central importance to narrative art were well under way: the practice of oral storytelling and the beginnings of dramatic performance.'[30]

Another specificity of the narrative tradition had been 'the sharing of materials and methods between three genres superficially discrete: the vernacular story, the classical-style tale and the theatre piece'. These links had been 'forged well before the thirteenth and fourteenth centuries, the period to which we can attribute the oldest extant specimens of full-fledged vernacular stories and plays.'[31] That said, Lu Xun's influential *A Brief History of Chinese Fiction* (1930), written not in the new vernacular but in *wenyanwen*, seemingly invents, or unwittingly exaggerates, the link between the *huaben* 話本 (vernacular story), which Lu understands to be a 'prompt book' for storytellers, and the emergence of vernacular written narrative.[32] While vernacular stories circulated, they were most probably not in book-form and 'had nothing in common with

x. Relatively speaking, Mao was not poor, but he was still a peasant's son obliged to work as a university librarian assistant to finance his studies.

so-called *huaben*'.[33] As Lu's friend Matsuda Wataru noted, 'in every case ancient occurrences of the word *huaben* could be interpreted as meaning nothing more than "story" or "story stuff"' and books or stories 'that qualified as such in the title are so called by modern editors probably under Lu Xun's influence'. Indeed, the existence of this type of 'prompt-book' is now dismissed as 'mythical'.[34]

Lu Xun was attempting to fill a gap, to invent a history of Chinese fiction, what he named *'Zhongguo xiaoshuo'* 中國小說 (China fiction). His Preface explicitly identifies as Chinese 'fiction'—or as he put it 'fiction of China' (*Zhongguo zhi xiao shuo* 中國之小說)—certain types of prose written over a period of 2,000 years or more: 'The fiction of China has hitherto had no history; if it has had, then it is to be found in histories of the literature of China written by foreigners'.[35] This is my translation; the authorized version by Yang Hsien-yi and Gladys Yang is as follows: 'There has never been a history of Chinese fiction, if we except the accounts of Chinese literature written by foreigners.'[36] The Yangs excelled as translators; I provide my own alternative simply to show the contrast between the more territorial 'China' (the only modern word used in Lu Xun's otherwise premodern sentence), and its official translation as 'Chinese'.

However, Lu Xun was right to point to the role of foreigners in the representation of what they unproblematically called 'Chinese literature'. As celebrated sinologist Herbert A. Giles (1845–1935) proudly boasts in the Preface to his 1901 *History of Chinese Literature*, 'This is the first attempt made in any language, including Chinese, to produce a history of Chinese literature'.[xi] While the word 'fiction' is not mentioned in the first

xi. Giles had been a British diplomat and was subsequently professor of Chinese at Cambridge for three and a half decades. Giles's book held five chapters (out of eight), in the sixth we learn that after 'the Drama', the 'second literary achievement of the Mongols' was 'the introduction of the Novel'.[37] Giles continues: 'The origin of the Chinese novel is unknown. It probably came from Central Asia, the paradise of story-tellers, in the wake of the Mongol conquest. Three centuries had then to elapse before the highest point of development was reached.'

For Giles, then, as for his predecessors and the collective European imaginary as a whole, 'Chinese' described not those who were hoping for and struggling to bring about a new nation-state with a new language and culture, but the 'native scholars ... [who] do not seem ever to have contemplated' producing the history of 'a literature which was already in existence some six centuries before the Christian era, and has run uninterruptedly until the present date'.[38] It would never have crossed Giles's mind that the contours of the territory containing this literature had changed many times; that the languages in which this literature was written were varied and had evolved over time; or that this literature was accessible only to an infinitesimal fraction of the Qing dynasty's subjects. In the nature of his project and in his attitude towards 'native scholars', Giles was a classic Orientalist: everything good and interesting in what the West had named 'China' was all in the past—a past that could only be entrusted to the Western sinologist.

As to his discussion of 'the Novel', whilst such Western sinologists had fallen into the habit of referring to long pieces of fiction from the Ming and Qing dynasties as 'Chinese novels', Cyril Birch advises that 'the category novel as such may be inappropriate ... prior to the twentieth century.'[39] The expression *xiaoshuo* 小說, literally 'small talk', referred to the 'popular'

sway for much of the twentieth century, despite being debunked by such noted Chinese critics as Lin Yutang 林語堂 and Qian Zhongshu 錢鍾書.

narrative—seemingly an 'entertainment' genre held in contempt by the scholar class, which at least overtly preferred the genres of refined prose and poetry. Fiction 'no doubt belonged to a minor tradition rather than the central elite culture of historiography, philosophical prose, and lyric verse.'[40]

It was only with the advent of Western terminology that the terms 'novel' (*changpian xiaoshuo* 長篇小說, literally 'long-length fiction') and 'short story' (*duanpian xiaoshuo* 短篇小說, 'short-length fiction') were coined; there was also the *zhongpian xiaoshuo* 中篇小說 ('middle-length fiction'), often translated into English as 'novella', and occasionally as 'novelette'. Types of modern, national-language fiction would thus be classified according to length. The appearance of the novel in the Western sense was also a product of the familiarity with foreign novels—including much middle-brow fiction such as the adventures of Sherlock Holmes and Jules Verne's science fiction novels—that were translated into the literary *wenyanwen* towards the end of the nineteenth century.[41]

Short fiction started to be written in the modern vernacular in the late 1910s, notably by Lu Xun, whose short story *Kuangren riji* 狂人日記 (Diary of a Madman) was written in April 1918. However, while Lu was writing in a sort of vernacular, it was not precisely what would become the national language. Moreover, he did not adopt a modern narrative style and *A Q* (阿 Q), written in 1922, may be seen as 'a contemporary parody of the traditional "story script"' or *huaben*, or at least what Lu Xun understood that to be':

> Not all the conventions are there, but some are, and this is the only story that Lu Xun [魯迅] wrote in serial form. Here again, however, *A Q* is the exception, and the *wenyan* [文言] (literary language) influence on Lu Xun's works seems to predominate.[42]

The first full-length novels in the national language only started to appear in the second half of the 1920s and the early

1930s. Better known for his poetry and drama, Guo Moruo 郭沫若 (1892–1978) published *Luoye* 落葉 (Fallen Leaves) in 1926; the novelist Lao She 老舍 (1899–1966), later celebrated for his *Rickshaw Boy* or *Camel Xiangzi*, published *Lao Zhang de zhexue* 老張的哲學 (The Philosophy of Lao Zhang) in serial form in 1926, and in book-form in 1928. The following year, 1929, the anarchist author Ba Jin 巴金 (1904–2005), best known for his 1931 novel *Family* or *Jia* 家, published a novel written during his time in Paris entitled *Miewang* 滅亡 (Destruction); in 1931 the feminist author Ding Ling (1904–86) published the novelette *Shui* 水 (Flood).[43]

The 'novels' that the young revolutionary elite set about writing were far removed in form and content from vernacular Ming and Qing fiction (1368–1911), and owed almost everything to the Western and Russian modern novel. The pre-existing vernacular language (*baihua* 白話) indicated the potential of a modern vernacular and national literature—one constitutive and representative of China the nation-state—but it was Western modern fiction that pioneering republican writers such as Lu Xun, Mao Dun, Ba Jin and Lao She took as their model.

***

As for the spoken language, we have seen that the new national language drew on the former lingua franca of officialdom, itself based on the colloquial language spoken in the northern half of the dynastic territories. It was the language known as *guanhua* 官話, literally 'official talk', or what in English we call 'Mandarin'. This bureaucrats' language had already undergone several transformations before emerging as the basis for the new national language. What was known as Nanjing Mandarin had served 'as the dialectal base of the lingua franca' from the fourteenth century onwards, and was the colloquial language of the state in the oral conduct of its affairs. From the middle of the nineteenth century, however, Beijing Mandarin was the dominant dialect: 'there was no attempt at codification or standardization of the lingua franca as a standard form of spoken Chinese for the general public. It was not taught at school ... The number of people who attained any degree of proficiency in it was minimal in areas of southern dialects.'[44] The term Mandarin is now, somewhat erroneously, applied to what is in fact *Putonghua* or Standard Chinese. Mandarin was a *spoken* language. But what many English-speakers now refer to as Mandarin is a variety of 'written-down Mandarin'—Standard Chinese, in both its oral and written forms.

As we know, when the Chinese Republic was established in 1912, in the absence of a formally codified modern national language, the new state's administration continued to employ *wenyanwen*, a written code that could be pronounced differently in different parts of what we now call China; that had also been adopted in Japan, Korea and Vietnam; and which differed little from the written language employed two millennia previously. This meant that, while the elite could communicate in writing and could read all the texts produced since the time of Confucius, local spoken, and largely unwritten, languages continued to be practised as mutually unintelligible tongues. Similarly, cultural expression of the non-elite was regional and popular, as instanced by local theatre traditions or, as the rest of the world knows them, 'opera', unintelligible to those not accustomed to the particular local culture and language.

Much interesting work has been done recently on local popular oral culture, in particular Vibeke Boerdahl's exploration of storytelling:

> From the time of the Song dynasty (960–1279), historical sources testify not only to the existence but also to the popularity in China of professional storytelling (*shuohua* [telling tales]).

> In the ever-growing urban centres, the storyteller (*shuohuade*) became an established figure of the marketplace and bazaar … Under the later name of *shuoshu* (telling of texts), we find a large number of local varieties of storytelling all over China.

This storytelling was in dialect and thus local, and as Boerdahl confirms Yangzhou storytelling in its own specific dialect 'was particularly famous':

> Among the storytelling parts belonging to different dialectal areas and different genres of performance, *quyi*—with or without music and percussion instruments—Yangzhou storytelling (*Yangzhou pinghua*) was particularly famous ever since the time of the first well-known Master of this art, Liu Jingting (1587–c. 1670) from the prefecture of Yangzhou. Because of his fame and later influence on several genres of storytelling in the Lower Yangtze area, he is generally considered the honourable father of Chinese storytelling.[45]

Given the specificity of this local-dialect oral tradition, and its inability to transcend linguistic borders, the author's insistence on calling it 'Chinese' storytelling is unfortunate. In contrast, it is interesting to note that in the Chinese title of Boerdahl's bilingual work there is no mention of 'China' or 'Chinese'. Unwittingly or not, the imprecise use of the words 'China' and in particular 'Chinese'—perhaps under pressure from peers or publishers to identify the object of study to the greatest number—simply perpetuates our collective inability to understand the diversity of China-Before-China and of China today. Within China itself, the intention of the authorities is clear, and recuperation of the local in service of the national culture is wilfully pursued.

However, some recent scholarship has begun highlighting this tendency to nationalize the hitherto resolutely local nature of popular culture. For instance, a study by Sylvie Beaud focuses on the impact on a local mask theatre practice, and its audience, of the 2005 film *Riding Alone for Thousands of Miles* (Qianli zou dan qi 千里走单骑) by renowned film director Zhang Yimou 張藝謀. Beaud writes: 'This event had direct consequences on the development of tourism in the region and on the cultural promotion of Guan Suo theatre [*Guan Suo xi* 關索戲], culminating in its 2011 recognition as a part of China's "national intangible cultural heritage" (*Zhongguo feiwuzhi wenhua yichan* 中國非物質文化遺產).'[46]

The film's title alludes to Chapter 27 of *The Romance of the Three Kingdoms* (*San guo yan yi* 三國演義), 'The Man with the Beautiful Beard Riding Alone for Thousands of Miles' (*Meiran gong qianli zou dan qi* 美髯公千里走單騎). The protagonist of the film is a foreigner, a Japanese retiree, who travels to the southern province of Yunnan hoping to film a mask theatre performance of this chapter. The film was made in Lijiang, which was developed as an 'ethnic' tourist location in the 1990s and was classed a world heritage site by UNESCO in 1997. However, since the local inhabitants—who belong to the Naxi ethnic minority (*Naxizu* 納西族)—were not renowned for mask theatre performances, the director, Zhang Yimou, imported a theatre company specialized in *dixi* 地戲, or 'earth theatre', a theatrical style specific to the neighbouring province of Guizhou.

Ultimately, very little of their performance is shown in the film. As for the Guan Suo theatre mentioned in the script, it does not appear in the film at all. And yet, due to outside interest in, and particularly online media coverage of, Guan Suo theatre, its heritage and tourism potential have been fully exploited. The Guan Suo theatre was appropriated by various regional- and national-level actors such that, ultimately, 'an essentially local cultural resource had become a part of the national heritage.'[47]

Zhang Yimou, in using a theatre troupe from another province, was evidently not overly concerned with the issue of authenticity. But then, for the international spectator, on whose ignorance the film-maker could count, the visual 'authenticity' would in any case be assured. As Beaud notes:

> [...T]he mask theatre is also used to construct an image of China as seen from abroad, notably through the gaze of the Japanese character. The film shows a naive and ethnic rural environment, which nevertheless holds the key to ancestral knowledge, the film-maker exploiting the aesthetics of the old architecture, natural surroundings, and the mask theatre. And yet, this stereotyped image of Yunnan also reflects the gaze of the Chinese themselves, since the province is advertised through similar icons (ethnicity, ancestral customs, lush flora and fauna, imposing landscape).[48]

Here, the gaze of the non-local Chinese—that is, Han-as-Chinese; Chinese minus the ethnic minorities—is tantamount to a sort of 'internalized exoticism'.[49]

Local popular culture thus loses what renders it local; what makes it special. In particular, the ethnicities which inhabit China see their customs and oral culture taken away from them, only to be given back as mere strands of national culture. In this particular instance—but it could easily be generalized to other artistic practices—what is at play is a 'vertical movement':

> Emanating from the national through an artistic production that speeds things up, generating in turn local-level initiatives, thus to 'go back up' to national level and the appropriate authorities for allocation of heritage status. This cultural practice de facto becomes part of the state's heritage, that every Chinese may appropriate.[50]

The sleight of hand demonstrated by Zhang Yimou in the filming and production of *Riding Alone for Thousands of Miles* is nothing new. Since the 1980s, films, TV commercials and video clips have exploited the visual exoticism of local cultures, while their oral and aural specificities have been muted. After all, foreigners cannot tell one opera or theatre form from another, and popular culture for the majority of consumerist China is simply the homogenized fare offered by officially-controlled, nationwide television. Visually it all looks the same, and once again, it's all Chinese.

What we now know as Peking Opera, or more properly 'capital opera' (*jingju* 京劇), had been one of several varieties of regional opera performed at court in the eighteenth century, and which flourished during the reign of Qian Long 乾隆 (1736–95). Features of different and diverse regional operas (Shanxi, Anhui, Hubei) were blended into *jingju*; while in the 'arias' the Hubei dialect dominated. But outside of the capital, local operas performed in local languages continued to constitute the visual and aural popular culture of regional audiences. Diversity reigned. Only the second half of the twentieth century saw the decline and virtual disappearance of opera as a popularly consumed art form.

In the 1960s and 1970s, official 'revolutionary' cultural policy eliminated capital and local operas from the stage in favour of the homogenized Revolutionary Model Opera performed in the national language, *Putonghua*. The operas figured amongst the revolutionary song-and-dance shows dear to Mao's spouse Jiang Qing 江青. They included not only operas, but ballets and even a symphony, and were known collectively in English as the 'Model Operas'; their formal title was the *Geming xiandai yangban xi* 革命現代樣板戲, the Revolutionary Modern Model Theatre.[xii] There were originally only eight models, also known as the 'Eight Model Plays', developed between

xii. Xi 戏 signifies any kind of stage performance or spectacle.

1964 and 1968. The eight comprised five revolutionary Peking operas, two ballets and one symphony.[xiii]

They were preceded in 1964 by the historical song and dance epic *The East is Red* (*Dongfang hong* 東方紅), which recounts the rise of the Chinese Communist Party from its inception in 1921 to the establishment of the People's Republic of China in 1949. The hero is Mao Zedong.

A film version was released in 1965, and visual and audio recordings would also be made of the Revolutionary Opera. The soundtracks would be played constantly in the workplace, in schoolyards, and on public transport throughout the 1966–76 Cultural Revolution. This culture-for-the-masses was literally inescapable. The films made of these 'models' were repetitive and rebarbative, but constituted the only colourful illumination of an otherwise monotonous everyday life. But these films were not merely propaganda instruments for Maoist ideology; they were also sui generis vehicles for the propagation of the national language.[xiv]

In the late 1970s, after the end of the Cultural Revolution, old-style Peking Opera returned to the stage, and China's opera troupes toured the world. However, its audience had aged. In the mid-80s there were official attempts to revive old-style Peking Opera with state-sponsored festivals in the capital, but by the 1990s all that remained were tourist-oriented performances in which acrobatics dominated. Snippets are now

xiii. Operas: *Taking Tiger Mountain by Strategy* (*Zhiqu wei hushan* 智取威虎山); *On the Docks* (*Haigang* 海港); *Raid on White Tiger Regiment* (*Qixi baihutuan* 奇襲白虎團; *Red Lantern* (*Hongdengji* 红燈記); and *Shajiabang/Sagabong* 沙家浜. The ballets were *The White Haired Girl* (*Baimao nü* 白毛女) and *The Red Detachment of Women* (*Hongse niangzi jun* 红色娘子軍); the symphony was *Shajiabang* 沙家浜.

xiv. With the exception of the opera *Shajiabang/Sagabong* 沙家浜, which existed in both *Putonghua* and Cantonese versions.

performed during television variety shows, but full performances of entire operas are rarely staged. The short-lived revival of Peking Opera succumbed to the competition of incipient, urban consumer culture and technology and the massive rise in television ownership during the 1980s. Possession of television sets per 100 Chinese urban dwellers had increased from fewer than five in 1980 to almost forty in 1988, and rural ownership was not far behind. By 1991, a television set was owned by one in two rural households, and by practically all urban households.[51]

Nevertheless, opera still visually evoked a nostalgic exoticism for Chinese and foreigner alike. It seemed a powerful emblem of 'traditional' 'Chinese' culture. But opera is also an oral practice, and while there was one particular type of homogeneous opera that held sway in the capital, there were numerous local operatic traditions in which the songs were sung in local languages. To the untrained eye, the costumes and face-paint might all look similar, but the singing and dialogue would have been impenetrable to all outsider audiences.

In 1996, the year before Hong Kong was 'handed over' to China, the entertainer Gao Feng's hit song *Da Zhongguo* 大中國 ('Great China', or, more ominously translated, 'Greater China') received a great deal of exposure on China's official airwaves, and the extremely popular video that accompanied the song exploited to the full the visual finery of the 'Chinese opera'. The first few seconds featured several scenes in which actors appeared in operatic costumes, their function being to provide national colour—the aura of authenticity. The 'female lead' of this music video resembles the lead of the patriotic, militaristic Peking opera *Women Generals of the Yang Family*; she twirls away from the camera in front of the Gate of Heavenly Peace and the huge picture of Chairman Mao that overlooks Tiananmen Square. The viewer does not see the Square itself; the camera is filming from that position.

Though the exoticism of Peking Opera is deployed visually, the video makes no attempt to represent the form musically. In fact, there is nothing to fix these actors as representative of Peking Opera rather than any other Chinese opera tradition. Like the Yan'an folk drums that are filmed in this video, the sound specific to the practice is absent. Given that each region has its own opera sung in its own dialect, only the visual can effectively represent a nationwide, national image to the country's viewers. There is a lack of specific musical references, so that the visual allusions to traditional music culture diverge from, and even stand in opposition to, the music that would normally be commensurate with them.[52] Thus are national imaginaries made.

At the beginning of the twentieth century, there was no national popular culture. There was a state-wide elite culture, but there had been no national culture because, in the modern accepted sense of the term, there was no nation. Of course, there were commonalities that spanned neighbouring regions, but there was no homogeneous popular culture over the whole territory of the future Republic. Indeed, there was no need for one. National languages and cultures are required when rulers deem it necessary to institute an imaginary—the handful of phrases, images and beliefs that constitute a commonly held understanding of a community—in order for the ruled to subscribe loyally to a common notion that goes beyond mere territory or sovereign; more importantly, so that they might fight and die for it.

Such homogenization is attained largely through violence and brutality. National languages—take modern French, for example—have only been arrived at, or rather imposed, by wilful central determination, and through the merciless eradication of local languages. In the twentieth century, the tendency of the modern industrial-capitalist state toward uniformity, centralization and rationalization was reinforced rather than challenged by Marxist ideology. The policies and mentality of the French Revolution—whose dominant faction, the Jacobins, insisted on the centralization and unification of France—were seen as exemplary. From a twenty-first-century perspective, we can see both positive and negative aspects, or rather emancipatory and oppressive tendencies, in the politics of the French Revolution. In order to assure the revolution's success and a real end to feudal and monarchical hegemony, a cultural revolution as well as an administrative one was needed. The language of Paris—in fact, the language of the court of Versailles—was imposed throughout France, and regional languages and customs, such as the differing legal tradition of the south, were prohibited. There was no intermediate or alternative position allowed. Regionalism was understood as reaction, as counter-revolution, as anti-modernization. For 200 years this ideological position has dominated the French national and popular imaginary.[53]

Beyond France, in the eighteenth and nineteenth centuries the example of the centralized nation-state became dominant. It was not limited to progressive thinkers, but rather was the dominant ideology of modernization and industrialization. This ideology was to have profound effects on the later development of Marxist thought concerning the state and the organization of culture—in particular, the thought developed by the traditional Communist and Socialist parties. Eventually, Marxist-Leninist parties would deploy this ideology to implement centralized, national cultural policies, and indeed culture would be instrumentalized as both a battleground for politics, and would replace economics as the engine for social and national progress.

Given this historical context, it seems almost normal that a similar ruthlessness should be practised in twentieth- and twenty-first-century China. Thus far, not only non-centralized languages that can be written with Chinese characters but also those unconnected to the Sinic language family, like Tibetan and Uighur, survive. Cantonese and the Wu language, spoken in Shanghai and its hinterland, are employed by scores of millions as a first language, despite official attempts to stifle and censor communication and creativity in these idioms; Cantonese is also the language of what Beijing sees as the fractious and contestatory population of Hong Kong. Local activists fought in the 1960s for its right to exist, and it was subsequentely promoted by the British state as the Chinese language of choice for the then colony.

Since 2010, however, there has been significant state curtailment of the relative latitude that has so far allowed Cantonese to exist as a language of everyday communication and cultural expression for over 60 million people in south-eastern China. Even in Hong Kong, where 97 per cent of the population speak the language, Cantonese is now under threat from *Putonghua*, which is ever more present as an official and everyday language of communication. In China itself, militating in favour of the maintenance of local languages is treated as seditious by the Chinese state. Witness the fate of Tibetan language advocate Tashi Wangchuk:

> 'A Tibetan's Journey for Justice', produced by *The New York Times* in 2015, told the story of Wangchuk's trip to Beijing to seek legal assistance in filing a lawsuit against local officials regarding the lack of Tibetan-language education in schools. It revealed that no law firm was willing to take on the lawsuit and that the state-sponsored TV station, CCTV [China Central Television], refused Wangchuk's request to report on the situation.[xv]

xv. Tashi Wangchuk was tried on 4 January 2015 after having been held in detention for two years. In May 2018, he was handed a five year prison sentence.

The police used this footage as evidence that he had deliberately incited 'separatism', supposedly by attempting to discredit the Chinese government's international image and its policies on ethnic minorities.[54]

Languages other than the official *Putonghua*, then, are seen as a danger to the drive towards absolute homogeneity. Meanwhile, their very existence gives the lie to the notion of a pre-existing, longstanding, unified, cultural entity called China.

8

CHINA-BEFORE-CHINA REVISITED

What in this book I call China-Before-China was unified administratively, and functioned through common textual and bureaucratic practices, much as the Habsburg Empire did. A unified state may well have existed over parts of what is now territorially China for much of the two millennia that preceded the founding of the Republic of China in 1912, but it was not a people's China, nor a nation, and even less a nation-state. It was a space occupied by peoples who displayed great diversity in their linguistic, cultural, social and religious practices. Beneath the level of the state's institutions, the only semblance of popular consciousness that extended across the entire territory was constituted by the various manifestations of the Buddhist religion which spread out of India and through China from the Han dynasty onwards. But Buddhism, unlike Catholicism, was not an organized religion that could be used to challenge the power of the state; and it could be woven into the stuff of local social practices.

China-Before-China, then, was a web of multifarious peoples with their divergent languages and customs, with only the distant State far above to hold it all together. The legacy of those local sociocultural practices (such as language) survives in twenty-first-century China, but of course today the cohesive force is provided by a nationalization of the territory and its peoples, achieved through application of what were once 'Western' sociocultural economic and technological systems, and which are now that incessant flow of planetary technological-economic magma we call 'globalization'.

To emphasize the distinction between China the nation-state and the past state and societies whose territory partially overlapped (what I have called China-Before-China) is not to deny or minimize the importance and richness of the heritage, both elite and popular, that past cultural practices have left to twenty-first-century humanity. I see this in a manner very similar to the way Castoriadis compared the relationship of Greco-Occidental cultural and intellectual history to modern forms. Just as Socrates, Aristotle and the Stoics are available for all to reuse, purloin, admire or disregard, so is the thinking of Zhuangzi, Laozi and Confucius available to all humanity, and not just those in China who would use them to reinvent the past so as to bolster a present national narrative. More than 2,000 years of artistic and other forms of creativity constitute a rich cultural resource for humankind.

Much of that creative practice even predates the unified state that was created by the Qin dynasty (221–206 BCE). Understanding and use of this common resource, as old-school Orientalist sinologists knew only too well, requires no knowledge of today's China—neither of its language nor of its society. You do not need to frequent a Confucius Institute in order to read Confucius. And yet the Chinese state today still attempts to nationalize, recuperate and package the practices, objects and texts of the past as instruments and evidence of its own present-day legitimacy, while on the contrary such practices and objects show today's China to be very young and very disconnected from the past.

One outstanding example is the use of archaeological finds to bolster present-day China's image as the inheritor of an enduring and continuous 'ancient' civilization. Witness the 2018 article in the Chinese government-sponsored English-language paper *Global Times*, 'Chinese civilization proven extra ancient.'[1] The Liangzhu 良渚 site, first discovered in 1936, 'proved what many Chinese have always wanted to believe and often speculated: Chinese culture is more than 5,000 years old'. In January 2018, China's government recommended the Liangzhu site as a candidate for World Heritage status in 2019. However, what the *Global Times* report fails to mention is the ethnic difference of the people who inhabited Liangzhu. According to an international team of scientists who investigated the DNA of human remains found on site, a 'high frequency of O1 was found in Liangzhu Culture sites around the mouth of the Yangtze River, linking this culture to modern Austronesian and Daic populations.'[2] Whilst the study puts in serious doubt the legitimacy and the 'purity' of the Han ethnic category, nevertheless, the team of scientists, eight out of nine of whom were Chinese, concluded in desultory fashion that their study shows 'the multiple origins of the Chinese Civilization'.[3]

It shows nothing of the kind. It demonstrates, rather, that multiple populations, arriving from different parts of the globe, for a time inhabited parts of the land mass we now call China. That does not make the Liangzhu culture part of 'Chinese civilization', any more than the prehistoric paintings dating from twenty-five centuries ago in the Pech Merle cave of present-day France's Occitania region can be said to belong to 'French civilization'. Once more, the temporally distant—here the 5,000-year old Liangzhu culture—and the ethnically diverse are recuperated to, and for, the present-day Chinese nation.

PART TWO

CHINA BECOMING A SPECTACULAR POWER

9

READING CHINESE

The Chinese intellectuals of the 4 May Movement—a moment of cultural agitation that followed China's humiliation during the Paris peace talks in 1919—thought themselves invested in a mission to create a new language, and through it a new culture, for a new nation. As we have seen, the pre-republican language was seen as an ill-adapted and unadaptable elite written language that embodied and represented all the constraints with which the newly emerged intellectual class wanted to break. This class was creating culturally a nation that had been imagined since the mid-nineteenth century.

The realization of that national imaginary began in the 1920s; thirty war-torn years later, the instituted imaginary—the result of that ambitious national project—included a really existing national, nationwide literature and culture for China. Even if there was still massive illiteracy; even if there was as yet no national popular culture; even if the majority of Chinese still only spoke and understood their own dialect of northern Chinese or an altogether different language, the groundwork had nevertheless been laid. A new literary and bureaucratic language had been forged and was available for wider use.

Though far from making China a superpower, the achievement of the republican period (1912–49) was remarkable. Despite civil war, the long fight against the Japanese invaders

(1937–45), and civil war again, the cultural nation-building went on. However, the 1949 founding of the People's Republic of China would lead the newly-created national language, literature and culture to be harnessed, hampered, distorted, censored and reduced to mere instruments of ruling power. Indeed, by the time the present author took his first steps in studying Chinese in the last year of Mao's decrepitude, contemporary Chinese culture was but a pallid and debased series of dictated practices unworthy of any nation, and even less of a revolution. Try as I might, there was little I could glean aesthetically from Communist-era cultural productions such as the Revolutionary Operas. What little cultural creation took place did so underground, out of sight and unbeknown to the outside world. Fortunately, the culture of the earlier republican era provided more than sufficient terrain for those interested in China's modernity and creativity. After the Cultural Revolution officially ended in 1976, there was a gradual rehabilitation of old writers and artists whom we in the West assumed dead; many of them, such as the novelist Lao She, were indeed dead, and thus were rehabilitated posthumously; they got back their rights and what was due them, so their families benefited. It was that generation's pre-1949 writing that had been the cultural fruit of China's emerging modernity.

As a young sinologist, I wanted to see that modernity given its due. I was attracted to a minority of European and US-based scholars who took a tack diverging from the old sinology, which was still very much invested in pre-twentieth-century culture. However, I also did not find what I sought in the recently emerged 'China studies'—a branch of post-World War II area studies focusing on China-as-an-object and examining China through a social science prism. Rather I was attracted to the creation of a sort of modernized sinology, one which would value and recognize the literature and language of the twentieth century. Like other Western postwar students of Chinese literature and culture, I sought to have China's twentieth-century culture taken seriously; we longed to create a third space beyond the 'contemporary China' of the social sciences and the 'Ancient China' of the sinologists. Our aim, then, was to permit modern language and culture to be studied with as much respect and diligence as that accorded to the so-called 'classical' language and culture.

In hindsight, I was in many respects misguided and mistaken. First, because it is not the fact of studying the old or the 'ancient' that is problematic, but how one studies it. The major problem in creating a space for study and dissemination of modern culture was not the pre-eminent status and prestige accorded to that which preceded China the republican nation-state—called 'Ancient China', 'Imperial China', 'Classical Chinese', in other words the bedrock of old-fashioned ideological sinology. This was only a problem insofar as the modern was perceived to have taken up the standard of a 'China' understood as a multi-millennial continuum.

If the language, literature and culture of modernity are taken for what they were and are—constituent parts in the construction of the Chinese nation-state—then there is no need to perceive the 'old' as an oppressive burden. Rather, 'what came before' becomes a source of reference and a well-spring of ideas for today's world, both those who are now 'the Chinese' and the rest of humanity. The old only becomes problematic when aspects of premodern culture are recycled as ideology to justify conservatism and repression of both the individual and society as a whole, as has been the case with Confucianism since the 1990s. But even then, when the 'old' is taken out of its context, manipulated and redeployed for contemporary ends, is it really still the 'old'? The past is always out of joint, out of context, with respect to the present; although historicism is loath to accept this verdict on the necessary anachronism of its practice.[1]

There were two real threats to this idealistic third space. The first was the very idea that it was possible or desirable to modernize sinology—to extend its remit into a study of twentieth-century culture. The second was the more generalized and global marginalization and deprecation of all literatures and cultures in the late-twentieth-century academic syllabus, to the advantage of the technical and the economic. Indeed, the attempt to open up a space for the study of China's twentieth-century humanities coincided with the period of 'sciencization' of the humanities in general. This, then, was not the most favourable of moments for a new appreciation of modern Chinese culture, and indeed by the time modern Chinese literary and cultural studies were staking their claim to academic respectability, the entire field of humanities was already being obliged to assume the mantle of scientism.

This utilitarian approach harmed not only the global study of China-as-a-modern-entity, but also the study of its modern culture. First, in the 1960s and 1970s, the social sciences gained the upper hand in the way things Chinese were studied and researched; later, in the Thatcher-Reagan era, business studies and the obligation to show the economic value of learning languages seriously damaged the study of twentieth-century Chinese humanities. Indeed, today in Europe, China studies—which includes most 'useful' disciplines and thus excludes culture—and 'business Chinese' form the overwhelming focus of studies relating to China. The study of literature and culture has become minor, and what learning of language there is has been entirely instrumentalized.

While I by no means advocate a return to the state of affairs that prevailed prior to the 1970s—when most older European universities neglected modern China altogether—what is now conjured up before university students' eyes is a mirage of a university course. Students are allowed, or even led, to believe that the newly minted graduate can 'do business' in China armed only with two or at most three years' cursory study of the spoken language, a few hundred Chinese characters committed to memory, and a facile recourse to mobile phone applications. The contrast is stark with the 'educated' Chinese, who might know 8,000 characters; a minimum of 2–3,000 would be needed to read a newspaper. Regrettably, the standard offer to Europe's students today consists of university courses that leave their graduates without knowledge of the reality of Chinese society, without even a desultory acquaintance with China's culture, and with a mere veneer of linguistic competence.

Even in China itself, as elsewhere, contemporary cultural consumption—I leave aside creation—is in the hands of the purveyors of visual-aural pleasure, and thus under the dominance of the image. Literary 'products', which must pass through the hands of the censor, constitute a small part of even the current Chinese middle class's consumption. In the academic realm, there is less and less access to critical thinking from outside mainland China; translated academic monographs are subject to both censorship and heavy editing.[i]

The situation regarding translations from, rather than to, Chinese is also far from idyllic. The choice of which titles get translated—one hitherto in the serendipitous hands of Western publishers and translators—is now subjected to a darker, less haphazard control: the Chinese authorities' targeted financing of non-Chinese translators working outside China. Translated texts are the non-Chinese-reading public's only source of

i. Several years ago I was offered the possibility of publishing my book *China's Lost Decade* in Chinese translation in China, as long as references to the Tiananmen Massacre and the events of 1989 were expunged; the book was a cultural history of the 1980s and I could only refuse.

access to Chinese literature. Thus control over what gets translated constitutes an essential part of the regime's 'cultural-diplomatic' control over the projected image of China. Chinese texts in translation also form the main gateway to China's culture—to say nothing of social scientific and economic documentation—for non-Chinese-reading students and scholars.

The Chinese language, beyond basic conversational Chinese, is difficult to master, or rather demands time and application. Few are prepared to devote themselves to the long and difficult apprenticeship required. Moreover, for young would-be students of modern exotic Asia, there are more seductive cultures on offer; cultures in which the image dominates. Korean television soaps and K-Pop, Japanese video games and manga are all highly seductive. Understandably in an image-dominated consumer society, non-Chinese youth, just like the young Chinese, are more receptive to the allure of spectacular, 'showy', popular cultures, than they are to the dull, staid fare promoted by China's political authorities and cultural establishment. European universities offering Japanese and Korean languages are for this reason besieged by 'clients', whereas Chinese, for all its being the language of the early twenty-first-century economic success story, is comparatively under-subscribed.[2] Twenty-first-century China so far has been a 'turn-off'.

My own apprenticeship of Chinese took place in London, at the specialist School of Oriental and African Studies (SOAS), then a constituent college of the University of London. The course was divided more or less equally into 'Classical' and 'Modern' Chinese. It had not always been so: a year or so before I started there, the undergraduates had demanded that the curriculum be more concerned with the modern and the contemporary. It was the 1970s—many students came to study Chinese because they were interested in the China of Mao, which had only just started to re-emerge on the international stage.

To an extent, the Chinese course at SOAS corresponded to the spirit and project of modernized sinology I evoked earlier. Demanding four years of text-based learning and much dictionary work, my studies were entirely linguistic and literary. 'Classical Chinese' seemed difficult. It was a dead language with inadequate dictionaries and grammars, and few translations; it was like learning Latin without the cribs. However, since China was still in the throes of the Cultural Revolution, in modern Chinese language classes we studied some revolutionary texts which were at the antipodes of the Confucian texts we studied in 'classical Chinese'.

Nowadays at SOAS, and I cite this institution simply because it was a beacon of Chinese and China studies for so much of the twentieth century, it is possible to obtain a Master's degree in Chinese studies having only pursued a one-year course. Moreover, the study of the language is not even obligatory, and in any case is only available as a minor. However, it is possible to study both modern and premodern literature entirely in translation. Thus, without ever having read a word in Chinese, one can be a 'Master' of Chinese literature. But then, in the marketplace that the English university has become, everything and anything is sellable and so possible. The Chinese authorities cannot be held solely responsible for the impoverishment of our knowledge and understanding of China.

At a moment in time when intellectual lethargy, or worse disinterest, has turned to complacency in the face of the onslaught of China's soft power, and when the economic interest of 'golden partnerships' is privileged over an increasingly harrowing human rights situation, never has it been so important to know the reality that is China—to read and understand what is said there, to be able to converse and communicate with the people(s) of China, and to regain our now lost appetite for so doing.

10

VERSAILLES

As we have seen, from the middle of the nineteenth century, the elite in what is now China felt itself obliged to reinvent the failing Manchu (Qing) monarchical state as a modern nation-state. The 1912 Republic's early failure to translate this instituting imaginary into a reality, and the denigratory manner in which it was treated by the victors of World War I at the 1919 Versailles peace talks, reaffirmed in the minds of this elite the need to emulate the West, as had Japan. After all, it was Japan, as a wartime ally of the UK, France, and the USA, that had succeeded in being treated as a major power at the peace conference table. China had also been an ally, and had sent men to serve on the European front in the Chinese Labour Corps digging trenches for the British and French and assuring logistics behind the lines; Britain's Royal Navy was also manned below decks by Chinese seamen.[1] But the Republic of China could not compete with Japan's military and, increasingly, economic might.

It was the now powerful Japan that swept the table at Versailles and 'inherited' Germany's colonies and economic rights in China's Shandong Peninsula; Woodrow Wilson's anti-colonialist policies were only applied to European would-be nations and not to Asia and Africa, where Europe, and now Japan, had their imperial interests. Japan had already been victorious in the 1894 war with the Qing state, prising away its influence over Korea and acquiring the island of Taiwan, and again showed its military superiority in the 1904–5 Russo-Japanese War. Japan had thus succeeded in imposing itself on the international stage after several decades of successful modernization, while the fledgling Chinese Republic had seen itself humiliated.

The lesson of Versailles seemed clear to China's eager young elite. To create for the first time this modern nation-state called China, it must emulate the West and even Japan. This process of nationalization, together with all the technologico-economic transformations it entailed, was seen as the only way to resist the global colonialist system that had just humiliated it once again, and to attain sovereignty over what must become a national territory. This was an ideological conviction shared with other colonized peoples. Sovereignty, it was held, could only be achieved by the institution of nation-states, which the Versailles process had just reaffirmed as the only form of organizing the world's peoples. Such nation-states were necessarily modern, both technically in the widest sense and economically. In other words, they had to become capitalist, or at least to pass through a capitalist phase; the dominant ideology of the time admitted no other way of being modern.[2]

A classical radical, or Marxist, reading of the outcome of Versailles would hold that the conference put the imperialist world in a dilemma and ultimately spelt its death-knell. The non-white, non-European world could not benefit there and then from the Wilsonian doctrine of self-determination, but the principle of the essential nexus between nationalism and modernity had nevertheless been reaffirmed and would, sooner or later, bring the decline and fall of colonialism.[3]

However, adopting this model of nation-state modernity as a means of self-determination and attainment of sovereignty was akin to taking up a poisoned chalice. Once the political and intellectual activists of what would be China had accepted the need for Westernization/modernization—let us recall that the term Westernization (*xifanghua* 西方化) was synonymous with modernization in the first half of the twentieth century—then China's incorporation into the world system of modernity became inevitable. Similarly, this chosen path obliged the Republic of China to adopt Western logics, which meant the jettisoning of extant knowledge and conventions that had hitherto been practised over two millennia by the dynastic elites. As we have seen, it also necessitated the discarding of popular linguistic diversity and cultural creativity, expressed in the various art forms, crafts, skills, ways and habits that had been practised locally in China-Before-China for centuries if not millennia. Anything that could not be appropriated for the national project was to be thrown aside, for to nationalize and modernize was to rationalize and homogenize.

It is disputable whether the Wilsonian doctrine of Versailles, and the Western imperialist system that gave rise to it, constituted the only possible strategy for what would become known in the Cold War era as the Third World. What is certain, however, is that the procedures of modernity, intimately intertwined with the procedures and logics of colonialism and capitalism, were taken to be the global panacea. Colonialism's greatest success at the start of the twentieth century, a success that continues to this day, was to have convinced colonized peoples, or rather their elites, that there was no alternative to the mimicry of this modern nation-state paradigm.

For the elite, what counted above all was access to the colonial powers' knowledge and their science. Yet, in the pursuit of this logic, an enormous contradiction was disregarded. In order to 'regain' sovereignty, or rather achieve a national power of agency for the first time, the China that was being created had to turn its back on everything within its territory that was local and heterogeneous. Rather than preserving and promoting the rich diversity to be found with the frontiers inherited from the Qing state, the nationalizing strategy required the homogenization of language, cultures and customs, and the elimination of diversity in favour of uniformity. In short, China, in order to become China, had to imitate, and thus inevitably become, the West.

Science and scientism took hold of the elite's imaginary in China as it had taken hold of the West's in the second half of the nineteenth century, when 'in the name of science it was deemed necessary to destroy false ideas, religions, cultural traditions, myths; all that was a product of the imagination of the dark ages had absolutely to be replaced by the Light of Science.'[4] While this logic is still dominant in the twenty-first century, with all its social, economic, and environmental consequences, it now clashes with the authorities' attempts to institute in global terms a national, identitarian cultural politics that denigrates 'Western' constitutional ideas so as to combat the temptation of democracy. This is despite the fact that this desire for democracy and the rule of law is largely understood in the Chinese dissident imaginary as Western, so-called liberal, democracy, or really existing 'democracy', rather than the total democracy that would entail a project of societal and individual autonomy.

11

WESTERN 'VALUES'?

In 2015 the Chinese authorities launched a campaign against 'Western values' in the academic sphere, as if they wished to cut off China's nose to spite its face; the campaign gathered pace in 2016–17. Similar campaigns had been seen before, in the 1950s and of course during the 1966–76 Cultural Revolution. But, in the 1980s, the 'Campaign Against Spiritual Pollution' and the 'Anti-Bourgeois Liberalization Campaign' seemed to go against the grain of Deng Xiaoping's project to liberalize China's economy, which many believed would imply a corresponding democratization of society. However, at the end of the 1980s, China's paramount leader made clear his position on the limits of China's emulation of the West:

> The struggle against bourgeois liberalization will last for at least twenty years. Democracy can only develop gradually, and we cannot copy Western systems ... Bourgeois liberalization would plunge the country into turmoil once more. Bourgeois liberalization means rejection of the Party's leadership.... The struggle against bourgeois liberalization is also indispensable. We should not be afraid that it will damage our reputation abroad. China must take its own road and build socialism with Chinese characteristics—that is the only way China can have a future.[1]

At the end of 2017, 'socialism with Chinese characteristics' had evolved into 'Xi Jinping Thought on Socialism with Chinese Characteristics for a New Era'. Two decades after Deng's declaration, the new supreme leader Xi (2012–) had hardened the political line, if such a thing were possible, and the newly appointed Communist Party propaganda chief, Huang Kunming 黄坤明, declared in the *People's Daily*:

> There are especially some Western countries who use their technological advantage and dominance in discourse that they have accumulated over a long period to peddle so-called 'universal values', trying to seduce people into 'taking the West for beautiful', 'being compliant with the West', so that they dilute or even abandon their own people's spiritual cultural identity. The report of the Nineteenth Congress of the Communist Party of China emphasized that culture is the soul of a nation and a people...[2]

But where do, and where should, 'Western' values stop? Where does 'Western' science start? At stake is not only what is projected as Western culture, in fact now a global culture, but also what is perceived as Western methodology. But are 'science' and 'culture' separable? Indeed, in any discussion of science and culture, the question of the specificity of culture, or more specifically of cultural creation, needs addressing. To do so, we must also address the relationship between economics and technology—the latter having ousted science from its nest like a cuckoo. It is evident that the economic strategy of growth is severely damaging our planet, and that there is an urgent need not simply to opt for sustainable growth, but to reverse growth and adopt the path of 'ungrowth'. As the French political scientist Jacques Ellul laboured to have us understand, achieving such an ambition will require a global cultural, or 'civilizational', revolution on the part of humanity.[3] In any case, without the collaboration and participation of China, such a project would be unattainable.

From the nineteenth century onwards, the Western-dominated world was in part forced and in part 'chose' to adopt a Western-originated organization of knowledge and culture. Japan chose this course. To what extent this was indeed a pragmatic choice, and to what extent it was a function of a colonization of minds, is also a question that begs discussion. Either way, in the cases of both Japan and China, as in parts of the world that were fully territorially colonized by nineteenth-century imperialism, Western cultural and institutional norms and forms were introduced alongside scientific and technological ones. Not only were the natural or exact sciences deployed to displace local scientific understanding of the world, but creative cultural practices were also reshaped and forced into foreign disciplinary categories. A simple example would be the modern Western forms of narrative: the novel, the short story. Since World War I, then, cultural practice has taken what was once a 'Western' path, and is now a planetary highway.

So when the Chinese authorities have lambasted 'Western values' during the Cultural Revolution, during the various mini-campaigns against Westernization in the 1980s, and more recently under the reign of Xi Jinping, what are we to understand?[i] That, while the form is Western, the content must be Chinese? But after a century of 'modernization'/'Westerni zation', of globalization, what does it mean to be Chinese? If

i. It has been calculated that between 1949 and the end of the Cultural Revolution in 1976 there were altogether fifty-five political campaigns, most of which were critical of intellectuals, of political factions suspected of opposing the Party line, and of those deemed to espouse bourgeois or Western values. Whilst many thought and hoped that the end of the Cultural Revolution heralded the end of the Communist Party's 'campaign' culture, the 1980s saw its rapid resumption.

we adhere to the old notion that China of the twentieth and twenty-first centuries is essentially the same entity as it was for the preceding two millennia—or five, according to Xi Jinping—then very little remains 'Chinese'. But if the idea is accepted that creating this 'China' was always the ambition of the modern nationalizing project, then mostly everything in the territory is indeed representative of 'China'.

However, the official fallacy is maintained of an essential 'Chineseness' that is somehow 'rooted' in a culture, in the past. There is nothing new in this schizophrenic desire to adopt Western technology to make China strong while 'preserving' this 'Chinese' essence. It was at the heart of the 'self-strengthening' (*ziqiang* 自強) movement that followed the mid-nineteenth-century Opium Wars. This movement sought to strengthen China by adopting foreign methods in both military and political organization and industry, and, as logically follows, in education; in other words, what Jacques Ellul calls *la technique*. This logic was summed up in the phrase *Zhongxue wei ti, Xixue wei yong* 中學為體, 西學為用 ('Chinese learning for the fundamentals, Western learning for the practical application'), which would become a widely-used slogan at the end of the 1890s.[4]

This strategy has been applied, sometimes spasmodically, ever since. But once again it depended on *Zhong* 中 being an established identity, a given, which it was not. It was only just starting to be made. China's cultural identity was no more than an identity limited to a small elite, expressed in a premodern language inaccessible to the largely illiterate majority. As we have seen, ordinary people's culture was local, oral and popular. It was only the elite that enjoyed a shared culture across a territorial space, administered by a Manchu class whose power depended upon it. Again, the creation of a 'nationwide' or national culture meant first creating a Chinese nation, which required in turn the creation and realization of a 'national' homogenized language and culture, commensurate with the demands of the 'modernized' world.

What is now called a 'return' to 'Chinese values', then, would imply the undoing of 150 years of political, social and cultural institutions and practices. A return to 'authentic Chinese' culture would mean a resurrection of a minority culture practised by an elite, and of diverse local cultures practised in local languages. In other words, national Chinese culture is irredeemably modern. However, there can be and has been a false return to so-called Chinese values, to an ideological logic, that was first challenged and overthrown a century ago by the 4 May Movement. Confucian 'values', not for the first time in history, have been redeployed and reinvented to strengthen and support totalitarian forms of power, both in China and in other Asian states such as Singapore.

There is a central question here regarding cultural practices, and whether they could or should be subtracted from the set of globalized practices that are now common to the whole world. Should the former colonized world keep the technology and 'return' to local Ur-cultures? In the twenty-first century, as in the past, what is called 'culture' is instrumentalized to identitarian ends, with tragic consequences. It is so in China, it is so in Europe. Such instrumentalization pertains to a politics founded on invented cultural identities, on national and even supranational identities. For instance, the French government exploits the French language in the hope of maintaining and extending its influence in the francophone and latinophone world; whilst China, through the teaching of its modern national language *Putonghua*, propagates a myth of an 8,000-year-old homogeneous 'national' culture and attempts to exploit and extend a sinophone sphere of influence.[5]

12

MODERN, MODERNITY, MODERNIZATION

EQUIVALENCE, TOTALIZATION AND BELONGING

Since the turn of the millennium, there have been attempts to broach the dilemma of modernity and identity in the context of modern colonialism's aftermath. For instance, in the field of postcolonial studies and related academic domains, there is a debate on 'intellectual decolonization'—a sort of second-stage decolonization beyond territorial, physical decolonization. For, as we have seen over the past half-century, departing colonialists leave behind not only problematic, improbable borders, a proliferation of flags and national armies, and Western forms of sociopolitical organization, but also the Western cultural practices and ways of thinking that are embedded in them.

Is it possible for a page to be turned? Or is the best that can be attempted to render postcolonial modernity more homely, somehow 'naturalized', while preserving its apparent advantages? Alongside the notion of decolonization of the mind, there has also been a debate focused on so-called 'alternative modernities'; this debate has taken place not only in the Euro-American academy, but also in the Chinese academy, where the idea of a specifically Chinese modernity has been advanced—one which would necessarily be a good modernity.[1] But of what does modernity consist? The answer is in part revealed in the arguments of those who critique its Westernness, and promote the idea of 'alternative modernities'.

The alternative modernities concept was posited and discussed in turn-of-the-century special issues of the journal *Public Culture*. This series, entitled *The Millennial Quartet*, addressed the questions of 'alternative modernities', 'globalization', 'millennial capitalism' and 'neoliberal culture', and 'cosmopolitanism'.[2] Since the 1980s, what *Public Culture* had 'aimed to elucidate was, in fact, ways to think the relationship between parts and whole', between 'the local and the global', 'the particular and the universal', 'the singularity of societies and the larger worlds they inhabited—a problem that characterized the modern'.[3] Harry Harootunian, who adopts a somewhat adversarial stance towards a number of the arguments advanced in *The Millennial Quartet*, reminds us that the term 'alternative modernities' was coined by the anthropologist Arjun Appadurai, who, nevertheless, rapidly came to prefer the term 'modernity at large'.[4] Through the category of alternative modernities, Appadurai wished to articulate a relationship between the local and the global, the particular and the universal, which would 'supply identity to those regions of modern Asia, Africa and Latin America which had always remained as vague silhouettes shadowed by the glare of Euro-America', and would 'free the modernizing experiences of these regions from carceral categories like imitation and modular supremacy, original and copy in order to demonstrate the achievement of equivalence but with a difference.'[5]

On the other hand, Harootunian saw alternative modernities, globalization and cosmopolitanism—'a multicultural and hybridized world'—as three figures of totalization, each indicating 'a form of utopian aspiration and desire to find shelter or a sense of belonging.'[6] But what indeed lurks behind categories such as modernity, globalization and cosmopolitanism? In particular, what is masked by the modern, modernity and modernization? For Harootunian, 'the door was opened to pluralizing the modern' only when the field of social sciences, followed by post-World War II 'area studies', employed the word 'modernity' to avoid naming capitalism and colonialism.[7]

As to globalization, with the hindsight afforded by the economic and political evolution of the twenty-first century, it now seems vain to have seen it as 'a domain of cultural heterogeneity' rather than an economic homogenizing process.[8] Indeed, what is globalization if not the continuity of a post-World War II process of Americanization? This was meant to introduce a form of technological-economic 'imperialism' that eschewed the methods and trappings of the outdated European model of territorial colonialism, but which had as its ultimate weapon military might and the threat of US intervention. Such has indeed been the modus operandi of US power since the 1950s and into the twenty-first century.

At the economic heart of globalization was the transformation of the planet into a global market for the consumption of goods produced by the USA, Western Europe and Japan. But, as with the desire of the colonized to modernize via the nation-state model promoted by Versailles, the colonized parts of the world—what Mao would term the Third World—were not content merely to be the exploited, a base for cheap production. By the end of the twentieth century, the former Third World, and primarily China, was consuming and not simply producing. The dilemma was that the economic model was 'naturally' and necessarily entwined with cultural practices and ideological control.

In China, one of the main everyday instances of cultural practice is eating. Eating and cooking, as with all other practices in China, have historically been local, dictated by different ingredients and varying tastes. For most of the twentieth century, the

West knew only 'Chinese' food. But by the twenty-first century the regional cuisines of China had arrived in the cosmopolitan citadels of the West. 'Chinese' cuisine does not exist—or rather, there never has been a generalized 'Chinese' cuisine. This only existed when seen from the outside: in the takeaway restaurants run by Chinese immigrants in North America and Europe.

Often the primary sense of 'consumption'—eating and drinking—provides the most prominent examples of cultural differences and their obliteration: McDonalds as the great culinary leveller of our tastebuds. And before 'cultural imperialism' as a critical category gave way to globalization, Coca-Cola-ization stood for the historical process of economic homogenization which was then synonymous with Americanization. In fact, what has become known as McDonaldization is a little more complex than it seems, and describes not only a process of globalization, but also one of its derivatives: what became known in the late twentieth century as 'glocalization'.

Globalization is now firmly entrenched in our imaginaries as the inescapable driving force of the twenty-first century. But is this process of planetary technologico-economic—and thus, inherently, cultural—harmonization, standardization or homogenization so modern and so recent? What we have to understand as globalization is not so far from a much older process. Here, for instance, is a passage which might well be describing economic and cultural 'globalization':

> The bourgeoisie has through its exploitation of the world market given a cosmopolitan character to production and consumption in every country ... it has drawn from under the feet of industry the national ground on which it stood. All old established national industries have been destroyed or are daily being destroyed. They are dislodged by new industries ... industries whose products are consumed, not only at home, but in every

> quarter of the globe. In place of the old wants, satisfied by the productions of the country, we find new wants, requiring for their satisfaction the products of distant lands…
>
> In place of the old local and national seclusion and self-sufficiency, we have intercourse in every direction, universal interdependence of nations. And as in material, so also in intellectual production.
>
> The intellectual creations of individual nations become common property. National one-sidedness and narrow-mindedness become more and more impossible, and from the numerous national and local literatures, there arises a world literature.[9]

The above is an extract from a text first published in 1848, *The Communist Manifesto*. At first view, it is not immediately clear whether Marx and Engels consider this march towards a global economy and culture a good thing, but the sense of the words that follow is quite transparent:

> The bourgeoisie, by the rapid improvement of all instruments of production, by the immensely facilitated means of communication, draws all … nations into [its] civilization … It compels all nations, on pain of extinction, to adopt the bourgeois mode of production; it compels them to introduce what it calls civilization into their midst, i.e., to become bourgeois themselves. In one word, it creates a world after its own image.[10]

Already over a century and a half ago, Marx saw economic globalization as an inevitable process. But did he foresee the commodification of intellectual and cultural creation, or 'production' as he would have termed it? While Marx understood the logic of capitalism, probably better than anyone in the mid-nineteenth century, what he did not foresee was the emergence of a post-bourgeois economy and the hypermodern technologico-economic colonization of culture and language.

At least from the perspective of a masculinist, white Euro-American world-view, Marx and Engels were true internationalists, who transposed and introduced with ease ideas and lexical innovations from one European language (German, French, English) to another. For them, the internationalization of the work and product of the intellectual could only be beneficial to progressive forces. These two titans of interventionist, politico-economic critique had correctly foreseen and predicted economic and intellectual globalization, although this came somewhat tardily, and only after a long dominance of national capitalist strategies from the late nineteenth century until the rise of post-World War II Americanization. However, the change in power relations expected by Marx and Engels did not happen, neither in the West nor in the Marxist-Leninist world, and the globalization of intellectual, cultural and informational 'production' has fallen totally under the hegemony of the technologico-economic. The national bourgeois economy may have been replaced by networks of global economic power, but the new form of power still uses a familiar strategy: 'it creates a world in its own image'.

Marx did not evaluate economic and cultural globalization as good or bad; he was against neither economic nor intellectual 'cosmopolitanization', as he called it. The world had to be extracted from its feudal misery: the town must replace the country, Nature must be mastered. Marx and Engels did not mourn the demise of the local, since, according to their analysis, the new global hegemony of the proletariat had first to traverse the historical phase of capitalism with the system of nation-states. And here we may begin to understand that China's leaders, ever since Deng Xiaoping returned to power in the late 1970s, have not in fact turned their economic backs on Marxism. They are firmly anchored within its teleological logic.[i]

i. However, as we have seen in the post-2017 stance taken by Xi Jinping and

Indeed, Chinese Communism was always firmly anchored in the Leninist desire to compete with and then overtake the advanced capitalist countries; the argument was over how best to achieve that ambition. 'Catch up and outdo' or 'catch up and overtake' (*dognat i peregnat* догнать и перегнать) had been a slogan of Lenin's at a time when his 'basic economic goal was to catch up with and surpass the major powers through industrializing as quickly as possible'.[11] In November 1929, Stalin redeployed the slogan during the First Five-Year Plan. Thirty years later, in May 1957, Nikita Khrushchev proposed the slogan 'Catch up with and overtake America!'

Mao Zedong, who had admired Stalin but suspected Khrushchev of revisionism, visited Moscow in November 1957 and said, 'Comrade Khrushchev told us that the Soviet Union can surpass America within fifteen years. So I suppose we [China] can catch up with or surpass Britain within fifteen years.'[12] With the launch of the Great Leap Forward the following year, the supposed time needed to catch up was shortened. In April 1958, Mao Zedong declared: 'It will not take as long as [we] supposed before to catch up with capitalist countries in industrial and agricultural production.' By June 1958, he was claiming that China would surpass Britain in three years and America in ten.[13] The slogan was *chao Ying gan Mei* 超英赶美: 'Outdo Britain, catch up with America'.

In post-Mao China, the focus on the peasantry and the countryside so central to Marxism-Leninism/Mao Zedong Thought was superseded by urbanization, industrialism and what had been called 'savage capitalism'. Indeed, Marx and Engels themselves were far from being hostile to urbanization, industrialism,

---

his propaganda minister Huang Kunming, the Communist Party's defence of cultural particularism is far from observing this particular Marxist credo.

mechanization—in short, modernization. And while they may have been critical of the brutality of the bourgeoisie, they were admiring of the progress inherent in the advance of bourgeois national and international capitalist modernization.

Let us examine one further paragraph from the *Communist Manifesto*, an extract that oozes disdain for the marginal and the unmodern, and which contains a famously disparaging turn of phrase referring to the peasant way of life. It is also a text that shows Marx's acute analytical prowess in his prediction of the twentieth-century economic, but also cultural, balance of power.

> The bourgeoisie has subjected the country to the rule of the towns. It has created enormous cities, has greatly increased the urban population as compared with the rural, and has thus rescued a considerable part of the population from the idiocy of rural life. Just as it has made the country dependent on the towns, so it has made barbarian and semi-barbarian countries dependent on the civilised ones, nations of peasants on nations of bourgeois, the East on the West.[14]

Here we are confronted simultaneously with the full power of Marx's critical capacities and with his ingrained disdain for the assumed backwardness and decadence of the 'Orient'. For Marx, like his philosophical predecessor Hegel, establishes an equivalence between what is termed 'rural idiocy' and the ignorance and the backwardness of the East. Such historically inaccurate and ill-founded prejudices are still sadly entrenched, 150 years later, in the postcolonial, yet still deeply colonialist, European imaginary, with regard to the now globalized East.

It is tempting to adapt those words of Marx and Engels. With a few modifications to take into account contemporary economics and geopolitics, we could easily apply this passage to the achievements, ambitions and current project of the Chinese Communist Party since the mid-1990s:

> *The Party* has subjected the country to the rule of the towns. It has created enormous cities, has greatly increased the urban population as compared with the rural, and has thus rescued a considerable part of the population from the idiocy of rural life. Just as it has made the country dependent on the towns, so it has made barbarian and semi-barbarian countries dependent on the civilised one, nations of peasants on *the nation-state that is China*, the West on the East.

Leaving Marx and Engels, who may have been unable to foresee the evolutive nature of consumer capitalism, it was only the post-World War II 'alternative' theorists such as Cornelius Castoriadis, and the even more marginal Guy Debord, who were able both to theorize and predict how the economic landscape would develop, and to see how power and its representations would evolve. Castoriadis rapidly understood that Marx extrapolated to the whole of history ways of thinking that were appropriate and applicable only to Marx's own historical era; that he subsumed the diversity of global social forms under a schema that made sense only in the context of developed capitalist society.

Guy Debord, in his now celebrated and oft-revived theory of *société spectaculaire* ('society of the spectacle' or 'show society'), analysed the nature of alienation in twentieth-century society.[ii] While frequently and reductively understood as a critique of manipulation of the image in modern society, Debord's 'society of the spectacle' theory went well beyond analysing the relatively restrained sphere of mass media. He focused on the impoverishment of daily lived experience, the increasing alienation and fragmentation of human existence. Thus the 'spectacle' or 'show'—the sum of the independent images and

ii. Significantly, the French word *spectacle* also translates as 'show', as in cabaret or theatre.

representations provided by modernity—serves as a substitute for real and full experience of life. Individuals separated from one another in everyday life find unity only in the passive contemplation of the image, a modern substitute for religion.

Of course, the core problem is not image and representation in themselves, but the society that has need of them. For Debord, there were two types of spectacle in the 1950s: the diffuse, represented by the 'liberal democracies' providing the illusion of choice; and the concentrated, represented by the authoritarian model of the Soviet bloc, China, Indonesia and so on, in which the spectacle is focused on a quasi-religious leader. In *Commentaries on the Society of the Spectacle* (1988), an analysis which foresaw the 1989 fall of the Berlin Wall, Debord described what he called the 'integrated spectacle', into which the two systems—diffuse and concentrated—had started to merge; to borrow and integrate features from one another. This 'post-Communist' phase of the 'integrated spectacle', whereby the New World Order replaced the Cold War, is what is now represented as globalization.

The show that was homogenization, totalization and globalization was also 'tweaked' to be less frightening. This 'dressing-up' became known as 'glocalization'. The term was first used in the late 1980s by Japanese economists writing in the *Harvard Business Review*, but was popularised by a sociologist, Roland Robertson, who defined it as the mediating, relativizing, or minimizing effects of local conditions on global pressures; the 'simultaneity of both universalizing and particularizing tendencies'.[15]

Whether presented as full-frontal globalization or harmonized glocalization, the question is not the Americanness or otherwise of the process. The reality is that, both in the sense of postwar economic neocolonization and in the sense of displacement of local sociocultural practices by globalizing tendencies, the process of Americanization may now emanate

Fig. 1: Chan Chun Lee photographed by Van Ralty, Liverpool, c. 1912.

Fig. 2: Liverpool Chinatown arch with the characters *Zhongguocheng* 中國城 written right to left.

Fig. 3: *La Jeunesse* 1:3 (15 November 1915), featuring a portrait of Oscar Wilde. Note the characters written from top to bottom or right to left, and not left to right as they are today.

Fig. 4: KFC, McDonald's and local fast food outlets, Canton, 2007.

Fig. 5: 'A Momentary Fantasy': a peasant in central Beijing, 2004.

Fig. 6: McDonald's, Hong Kong chain-stores, and billboards for glocalized wedding photographs, Canton, 2007.

Fig. 7: 'One World, One Dream': Beijing Olympic Games slogan, 2008.

Fig. 8: 'With one heart build together the dream of a strong military', Huangpu, Guangdong, June 2018.

from America, Japan, France, or China. What matters are the processes of the 'Americanization' of everyday life that have long since embedded themselves in, and transformed, local imaginaries and local realities. I have Taiwanese students who grew up with McDonald's; indeed, the first McDonald's this author ever visited was in downtown Taipei in 1978. For these students, American fast food culture is already a long-normalized part of Taiwanese life. Both in Taiwan and on mainland China, there are 'home-grown' local and 'glocalized' fast food restaurants using the same system as McDonald's (see Fig. 4). Nevertheless, it cannot be denied that culinary taste and ingredients are challenged and transformed by foreign, imported, 'global' practices. I have taught mainland Chinese students who believe that milk products are an integral part of traditional Chinese culinary culture. It was fashionable for a time in the 2000s for restaurants in China serving regional cuisines from around the country to offer milk and milk-based drinks with the food.

The tendency to mask the global and normalize it as local is not limited to the national level: it has also reached the marketing strategies of the hyperlocal. For instance, national or even transnational—or rather supranational—television, radio and Internet-based news and entertainment services can and do produce community-level news packages that are tailored to local sensibilities. Or they may simply give the impression of so doing.

How then do nation-states, how does the national, cope with or negotiate these planetary homogenizing and totalizing phenomena? Is the national doomed to be subsumed and eclipsed by the global? No: it is very much imbricated in the processes of globalization and glocalization. The national continues to exist, in the sense that the product distributed and consumed by all those within the national boundaries becomes the great leveller—the grand homogenizer within the nation-state's boundaries.

In Chinese shops and supermarkets there are foreign products, such as milk-derived products, produced by multinationals like the French-based Danone. These are, of course, global products, that are sometimes glocalized. And yet, the French supermarket Carrefour distributes both non-Chinese and Chinese products in its China-based supermarkets. What matters is not what is consumed, but the pattern of homogenized consumption; what is important is that what is consumed is consumed all over China, or at least, for now, all over urbanized China. In other words, the consumption is national.

For local holders of power, this is the global at the service of the national. Indeed, the process of globalization is essential to the completion of older national projects. In China, the standardization of distribution and consumption since the beginning of the century has taken forward, and helped to complete, the project of technical and cultural nationalization, launched much later in Asia than in Europe. To recall Marx, like the European bourgeois society that preceded it, the consumer of America has created 'a world after its own image'. McDonaldization, then, may be understood as the final phase, the accomplishment, of nationalization in the ex-Third World; in the BRICS. Glocalization has merely served to lend the process of McDonaldization even more easily to projects of nationalization.

American, European and Japanese postwar economic dominance has been effectively challenged, by those who have emulated that process. But while American hegemony may have been threatened, cultural heterogeneity remains a chimera. As the Comarroffs demonstrate, the slippage from modernization to globalization relates to an economic process, and while 'modernization theory was based on the regime of production … the new world of globalization affirms the order of consumption'—a consumption predicated upon homogenization in form and, at times, on illusions of heterogeneity in content.[16]

What Harootunian writes about the nation-state in general is particularly relevant to my arguments concerning the Chinese nation-state:

> it had always been the nation's purpose to materialize a 'spiritual essence' capable of securing national unity through a number of ceremonial devices and practices supplementing the [state's] obligation to provide welfare and order. The nation half of the hyphen always aimed to make visible in diverse practices its concealed, 'mystical' side, while the state apparatus was initially pledged to furnish efficiency in the name of rationalizing the 'domination' of everyday life and progressive disenchantment. In this regard, the nation form came to resemble the commodity in both appearance and performance ... [Throughout] the semi-colonized and emergent national societies before World War II that encountered the force of capitalism and its destruction of received cultures of reference, thoughtful people were moved to resuscitate what was being lost—traces of an authentically *different* 'national life' derived from remote antiquity and which were made to anchor identity in the modernizing maelstrom.[17]

However, while this may have been the case for European and Japanese national societies, in the case of China, 'received cultures of reference' were neither national or popular, but the heritage of an elite whose cultural geography mapped onto the state's territory. There was no 'authentically different "national life"'; indeed national life was being busily created. Of course, the creators of China the nation would reclaim 'remote antiquity' for the national imaginary. But in order for 'bourgeois intellectuals to preserve emblems of their own culture', and to embed 'remote antiquity' in an imagined national culture, that culture, the 'culture of reference', had first to be created, as Clunas has shown in the case of 'national' painting.

The 'historic task' that the early-twentieth-century intellectuals of China's emerging bourgeoisie set themselves was an iconoclastic one: on the one hand, the destruction of the millennia-old elite culture of the old state, which concerned only a miniscule minority of the population; and on the other, the complex creation of a truly national culture for the new state. The immediate contradiction requiring their attention lay in the new literary culture's reproduction of an elite literature inaccessible to the majority, and the political need to create a nationalizing popular culture on the basis of the existing local entities. As for the 'desire for authentic values', the search for 'traces of a lost past' would come, but only later in the century.[18]

In terms of the difficult question of decolonization of the mind, there is the problem of autonomy and agency. Unless one argues that China's intellectuals, new elite and political class were entirely in thrall to Western capitalism, and this was clearly not the case, then it must be accepted that Westernization (*Xifanghua* 西方花), as modernization was known in the 1912 Republic, was a conscious strategy. The question then arises: was there the possibility of choice, was there room for agency? In other words, was the mind colonized, or should we accept that the new elite's desire to modernize, in other words to Westernize, was dominant, and that Westernization as a major component of the national imaginary was hegemonic? If Westernization is merely a synonym for modernization, which in China's case it literally was, then it merely constituted a façade for both capitalism and the colonialism that still held even the new China in its thrall. National salvation, the aim of more than half the globe in the post-Versailles era, depended on having a nation to save. In China's case, as for many other twentieth-century aspiring nation-states, this implied first creating that nation—creating a national imaginary to inhabit the shell of the new Republic—and secondly pursuing the technological-economic development that, it was believed, would lead to real sovereignty. This was a strategic course ridden with contradictions and complications. If choosing it was tantamount to minds being colonized, then there was indeed a collective colonization of the mind.

Rather than decolonization of the mind, Walter Mignolo writes of 'epistemological decolonization'.[19] The example he gives is 'the restitution of Amerindian philosophy of life'. But again, who invented or constructed the category of 'Amerindian'? Is there but one (timeless?) homogeneous 'Amerindian' philosophy? To talk of 'Chinese' philosophy is just as problematic, especially in reference to the clutch of competing schools of thought in China-Before-China 2,500 years ago. I am thoroughly convinced that thinking that would be useful to humanity today exists in the texts which survive from that time, retrospectively called Taoist.[iii] However, the notion that such thought could form the basis for an alternative, decolonized and 'authentic' Chineseness casts us into the realm of fantasy, which would make possible the worst kinds of manipulation; witness the reactionary usage to which the recuperation of Confucianism has been put since the 1990s.[iv] And if one were to restore the philosophy of an elite living nearly 2,500 years ago, in a cluster of small states within a small part of what we now call China, to whom and in the name of what

iii. Such as the *Daodejing* 道德經, *Zhuangzi* 莊子, or *Liezi* 列子.

iv. Once again, as I have attempted to demonstrate, only superficially does the language of this philosophy bear a resemblance to the language practised in China today. To be able to read the original would take almost as much effort for a Chinese person as it would for them to read Plato in the original. The only apparent advantage for someone brought up reading modern standard Chinese, and one shared with the Japanese, is that the script seems familiar; and yet often these seemingly familiar words are what the French call *faux amis* (words in a foreign language that look familiar, but whose meaning is totally different), and as we have seen the grammar is absolutely distinct.

would it be restored? In the absence of time travel, this philosophy can only either serve the purposes of the state by reinforcing its legitimacy, or serve humanity as a whole, as does the thought of Plato and Socrates. What it cannot do is 'return' China to some non-existent, pristine and primary condition of authenticity.

Given the recent integration of China into a global technologico-economic system, by 'decolonization of the mind' we might mean something more than simply becoming conscious of an enduring process of intellectual colonization. What, then, does 'decoloniality' mean? And how could meaningful decolonization be achieved? Could Western forms of the state be abandoned? Could modern military organization be given up? If the prospect of abandoning these technical and technological 'gains' seems remote and unthinkable, why does it remain thinkable for states to seek to establish cultural norms based on identitarian, xenophobic, or racist ideologies of cultural specificity?

Despite attempts to liberate postcolonial polities from the charge of imitation, the historical reality is such that modern 'national' cultures were, and are still being, created out of Western-inherited institutional norms and forms such as the nation-state, whose validity was universalized and enshrined by Woodrow Wilson at the same Versailles conference that led China's students to demand democracy and science. Without a modern nation-state, there would be no modern national culture; nor would there be a need for one. It will be recalled that students contesting the weakness and betrayal of China's delegation at the peace congress held up banners supporting the activist Chen Duxiu's call for Mr Confucius to be replaced by Mr Democracy and Mr Science: 德謨克拉西先生 *demokelaxi xiansheng* and 塞恩斯先生 *saiensi xiansheng*.[v]

v. See Zheng Wang, *Women in the Chinese Enlightenment: Oral and Textual Histories*,

As we saw earlier, women were exploited in the representation and creation of the nation, as they had been before the founding of Republican China, and as they continue to be in today's PRC. The sexism implicit in the figure of the two Misters is striking and unfortunate. That Western democratic institutions and the right to vote were withheld from women, and that with very few exceptions the world of science was a male preserve, may have made it seem 'natural' to personify the two demands as men—and yet, the reality was that numerous women students were at the forefront of the 4 May Movement. In fact, in the fight against a patriarchal ideology that not only obliged the young to venerate the old, but treated women as almost worthless, women were amongst the most ardent agitators.[vi] Indeed, the earliest radical ideologies in modern China were not articulations of Marxism, but rather of feminism and anarchism. Anarchism fuelled the nascent leftist movement with revolutionary ideas only to be subsumed under the ideology of the Communist party, while feminism—the early writings of Ding Ling 丁玲 (1904–86) were a fine articulation of feminist concerns—was likewise swallowed by the dominant, universalist, Communist-nationalist revolutionary ideology.

Berkeley, CA: University of California Press, 1999; Gail Hershatter, *Women in China's Long Twentieth Century*, Berkeley, CA: University of California Press, 2007; and Arif Dirlik, *Anarchism in the Chinese Revolution*, Berkeley, CA: University of California Press, 1991.

vi. Note how the two words were commonly transliterated in Mandarin from English: *demokelaxi* and *saiensi*. Later, 'democracy' would be translated *minzhuzhuyi* 民主主義 from the Japanese *minzhu* 民主 (people-rule), and 'science' *kexue* 科學 from the Japanese *kagaku* 科學. In Chen Duxiu's earlier, 1915 'Call to Youth', the Japanese-derived *minzhu* 民主 was preferred. It is possible that in post-Versailles China, when Japan had just been handed Germany's colonies, it was deemed preferable to avoid Japanese translations of Western terms.

But what exactly did Chen mean by 'science'? This future, and first, leader of the Chinese Communist Party saw science as the positivist cure to ancient obscurantism. For Chen, 'modern Europe's superiority over other races is due to the rise of science'.[20] Scholars, ignorant of science, were but charlatans using geomancy to hoodwink the people; farmers were ignorant of seed selection techniques and the use of pesticides; industrialists' ignorance of science was responsible for dependence on foreign countries; physicians were ignorant of anatomy, bacteria and contagion, and depended on ancient formulae such as *yin* and *yang*.

The solutions to such deficiencies was then obvious: 'As for such unknowledgeable thinking, such illogical beliefs, if we wish to cure them at the root, we apply science'.[21] In this denunciation of superstitious practices and old knowledge that not only constituted, but propped up, a conservative regime's ideology, Chen also opposes science to the spontaneity and creativity of the 'imagination'. Indeed, the sixth section of his 'Call to Youth' is entitled 'Scientific and Not Imaginative' 科學的而非想像的. For Chen, imagination is the antithesis of reason: 'In former benighted times there was, and today among uncultured peoples there is, imagination but no science. Religion, art and writing, were the product of the era of the imagination.'[22]

Disturbingly, Chen assigns imagination, here closely associated with myth and creativity, to the past. For him, there can be no cohabitation between science and imagination; rather, as in his celebrated slogan, he would pair 'science' with 'democracy'. Chen would soon abandon 'democracy' in favour of historical materialism, but his belief in science that could bring 'modernization' to China would endure. And yet, it is now evident from the catastrophic outcomes of the twentieth century that science, beholden to technology, was not the instrument by which democracy, in Chen's sense of liberty and autonomy, would be brought about. Witness the state of today's industrialized planet, of which China is an integral part. Science has not been objective, and has certainly not been neutral. And democratic control of science and technology remains a dead letter. Neither liberal democracies, nor totalitarian autocracies, are any longer the drivers of technology—they are the driven. The so-called neutrality of science has allowed a headlong and limitless expansion of unnecessary, and certainly ill-considered, technologies, which have not brought about 'progress', but rather a devastated environment and a socio-economically unequal global society.

13

CHINA AND THE GLOBAL TECHNOLOGICO-ECONOMIC SYSTEM

After the extreme capitalist conditions that urban China and, in particular, Shanghai had known in the 1920s–40s, the country's Communist leadership installed a Soviet-style state-capitalist regime after it took control in 1949. The split in the Communist Party between those Mao and his clique would call the 'capitalist roaders'—including Deng Xiaoping—and those clinging to a military-revolutionary mentality led to the Cultural Revolution (1966–76), a means for Mao to regain lost political power, and a temporary suspension of the movement towards full-fledged capitalism. The kind of flamboyant capitalism that China had already known under the 1912 Republic was thus put in abeyance from the 1950s until the 1980s. Particularly in the 1960s and 1970s, everyday life had been mundane, monotonous and spartan, and it was thus relatively easy for Deng Xiaoping, after he regained and consolidated power in 1976–8, to seduce the population with the colour and plenty of the capitalist enchantment they had lacked.

Capitalist modernity does indeed enchant, as the German thinkers Walter Benjamin and Siegfried Kracauer understood. Whereas the sociologist Max Weber announced that modernity had brought about the demythification and the disenchantment of the old social world, Benjamin saw industrial capitalism as having re-enchanted the world through the reactivation of mythic powers. This took place through the generalization of the mass-produced image, as with advertising billboards and their slogans, through which commodities could be displayed and shown off. The new heroes and muses were now cinema stars and the fictional characters of advertising posters. And it was Kracauer who taught us to apprehend the '*mise en scène* of commodities' that rendered visible and readable the abstraction that was, and is, modern capitalism.[1]

It was precisely this '*mise en scène* of commodities' that had been lacking in the humdrum day-to-day existence of the cities, to say nothing of the countryside, in Mao's China.[i] While Mao had done his best to put himself *en scène*, the people's everyday life was a grey existence. Even grass and flowers had been eradicated from the urban landscape because of their bourgeois connotations. This monotony had been temporarily relieved for the urban youth by the exhilaration of the Cultural Revolution's early years, when as Red Guards they had been handed the power and licence to overturn the stodginess of ordinary life by smashing and grabbing, and settling scores with their bureaucratic elders. But, when they had served their purpose, the ultimate authority sent these young militants off to the countryside to be 're-educated' by the peasants.

In the pre-Communist period, urban China (notably Shanghai and Canton) knew the enchanted modern dreamscapes described by Benjamin and Kracauer; it had temporarily forgotten the widespread misery and invasive alienation that must be paid as the price for industrial capitalism's glittering façade.

i. I recall a large window display at the main department store on Beijing's Wangfujing shopping street in late 1979. A small crowd had gathered to gaze at the television set, washing machine and refrigerator displayed in the window. None of them were then for sale; the display was merely a promise of what was to come in consumer China.

The boredom and alienation of the Cultural Revolution had left urban society thirsty for what it had missed. For the rest of the population, apart from the grandiose, staged, spectacular parades on the squares of China's major cities, there was little relief from the featureless tedium of daily life even during the Red Guard period.

Popular political optimism accompanied the return of capitalism in the 1980s, a decade of hope during which most enlightened people expected burgeoning economic liberalism to 'naturally', automatically lead to democratization and enhanced freedom of expression. Indeed, sporadically, haphazardly, there was some freedom. But then the realities of market economics started to become clearer. Liberal political dissent was rife in the intellectual classes, and social unrest was sharply illustrated by the millions of former peasants who had sought work in the cities but who were now suddenly unemployed, dispossessed and desperately roaming the country in search of work. Against this backdrop, the edifice cracked and Deng Xiaoping set things straight. After the Tiananmen demonstrations and the massacre on 4 June 1989, and after the collective shock had begun to abate, Deng relaunched his market capitalist initiatives, but this time with no illusory promise of political freedoms. 'To get rich is glorious', Deng had announced in the 1980s; now, in the 1990s, getting rich was the only means available to acquire a modicum of autonomy in one's daily life.

The endemic despair that infused Chinese society after the debacle of Tiananmen left little alternative but to smother desires and hopes of societal autonomy under the merchandise and enchantments of consumer capitalism. Following the hiatus during the revolutionary phase of Communist rule (1949–76) and the mirage of political and social autonomy between Mao's death and Tiananmen (1976–89), the way was now paved for China's reabsorption into the world's technologico-economic system. China today is as bound into the latter as the rest of the planet. The idea that a national Chinese 'identity' could now be preserved or resuscitated by the promotion of an identitarian cultural politics is illusory; even a majority of its own intellectuals regard this notion as sterile. What constitutes such an identity? Apart from a flimsy, mediatized political discourse, which rails against the West's 'universal values' at the same time as urging the population to engage in ever greater consumption.

Since the 1970s, China's leadership has yearned to be present everywhere on the world stage, and it has succeeded in the first decades of the twenty-first century not only in fully integrating China into the world economy, but also in ensuring China's presence and participation in the full gamut of the world's mediatized, spectacular circus: tennis championships, Formula 1 racing (the Shanghai Grand Prix), hosting the Beijing Olympic Games (2008), high-speed trains, the Chinese space programme. Even in the realm of woman's place in society, the ultimate retrograde denigration and commodification has been sought and won; for while the West's 'universal values' might be unwelcome, its masculinist and sexist values have been embraced and promoted through China's participation in the Miss World and Miss Universe 'beauty' competitions.[ii]

We have already explored at length the integration and negotiation of Western cultural and artistic practices into the cultural life of twentieth-century China.[2] Though the epistemology, literary genres, and cultural practices adopted from the West have remained Western, there were always in the twentieth century attempts at adaptation. There was nuance and dexterity introduced in the process of intertextuality, in

ii. In 2007 Zhang Zilin 张梓琳 became the first Miss World from the PRC, and in 2012 Yu Wenxia 于文霞 the second.

the practice of borrowing and embedding Western ideas and texts, resulting in a more or less imaginative and new 'Chinese' creativity. But official China's current participation in these 'ludo-economic' spectacular, global events reveals no attempt at mitigating, modifying or negotiating Western practices and institutions, and certainly no attempt either to reject or contest them, or to provide alternatives. This is despite the periodic tirades and campaigns against so-called Western values. Indeed, China is now fully integrated into economic, technological, spectacular global modernity. Moreover, China is in large part now responsible for generating and perpetuating 'Western' practices and institutions.

Elsewhere I have described this process, and this moment in time, as China turning the handle of a barrel organ. If I used this metaphor it was because it seemed best to sum up China's predicament today. The PRC's authorities are at the controls of a system that emits music according to a pre-established programme. It is a closed system, a technologico-economic machine which can be made to go faster or slower, but whose tune cannot be changed.[3] The organ-grinder produces a programmed melody, where the only variable that the organ-grinder can introduce is the speed at which the handle is turned. This is a systemic instrument created in the West, like the process of 'Americanization' that preceded it; it can be taken up and operated by any player 'willing' and powerful enough to accept the challenge.

However, is 'will' truly exercised? Does the organ-grinder ultimately have any more autonomy than the monkey chained to the organ? The repetition, stability, and inevitability of the barrel organ is akin to the system that subjugates and dominates us all in today's world, the 'technological system'. More complex than a simple barrel organ, the system nevertheless reveals itself through the interdependence of its components, through its generalization and through its acquired stability—the system seems so stable, widespread and entrenched that there is seemingly no way to reverse it, alter its course or stop it.[4] The handle continues to turn, and currently it is being turned by China.

If China's turning of that handle is a function of its inherited intellectual colonization, then how would or could the decolonization of the mind that we have already evoked take place? When decolonization is mooted, it conjures up an attempt to redress wrongs done to those territorially colonized in the past few centuries, in Asia, Africa, and Latin America. First they were colonized by physical force; then a politico-economic system was imposed; then they were left to deal with the aftermath of territorial decolonization as best they could: decolonized maybe, but still dependent.

Has the moment not come to consider some wider form of decolonization? Is it perhaps time to consider a decolonization not just for those who find themselves in the former Third World, but also for the rest of humankind? Ultimately, we are all now in thrall to the technologico-economic system that colonialism played a part in creating. Is not the decolonization that we need now the global decolonization of a collective mind convinced that there is no alternative? Would not a decolonized mind today entail not a return to some non-existent, imaginary, supposedly lost past, but rather a mind liberated to face collectively the ravages and excesses of the global technologico-economic system? Surely what intellectual decolonization ought to signify today is not a return to a mythic past, but a freeing of minds from that system's ideological colonization, so as to imagine and create a new human society and culture for a common future.

Now that the technologico-economic system has become planetary and generalized, China finds itself in large part responsible for turning the handle for us all. This is the historical logic that results from nineteenth- and twentieth-century colonialism, from the colonization of China by Western science and the ideology of Versailles, and from China's elite's embracing of such a path as the only means of survival and 'regeneration'—what the Chinese authorities recently have referred to as 'renewal'. The idea of renewal presupposes that there was formerly a country, nation-state, or polity that was China, and in the minds of the late-nineteenth-century elite, this was the case. Indeed, China's attachment to the 'science' that has led to the current technologico-economic system dates from its humiliation during the mid-nineteenth-century Opium Wars. So, while Deng Xiaoping's post-1978 reforms reconnected China to, and reinforced the logic of, the global model, they did not constitute its starting point. As we have seen, the dream among China elite's of being part of this planetary system stretches back to the dying years of the Qing dynasty. However, the present novelty is due to the national wealth created by the capitalist turn that was effected by the authorities after the 1989 Tiananmen massacre. It has supplied the conditions of economic growth which in turn have permitted the expansion of the technological system.

From the point when China rejoined the world technological-economic system in the 1980s, it was bound to imitate, reiterate and finally overtake the West, and thus to take over the handle of the barrel-organ. And yet, this 'taking-over' is illusory. The fact that sensational technological discoveries and advances are starting to be made, and will continue to be made, in China and not just in the West is without great consequence. Whether Chinese taikonauts rather than American astronauts will be the first humans to set foot on Mars is insignificant. Either event would be a logical consequence of China having inherited control of a machine it must continue to drive; a 'reasonable and normal consequence', as Jacques Ellul would say, of 'what already exists'.[5]

As early as the 1980s, Ellul, in analysing China's modern political history and the Chinese authorities' policies, showed an astute perception shared by few professional China-watchers. He foresaw both the technologico-economic and the political trajectory of the subsequent decades thus:

> The technical as both model and ideology has borne its first fruits in the notable quality of young Chinese scientists and technologists whom we host now in the West where they come to hone their skills and find their feet … The current [ideological] orientation is in line with reality. But it also expresses this reality, that the technical has finally vanquished the revolutionary model of Chinese communism. This interpretation allows us to avoid a frequent error that has gained momentum over the past three years [since 1979]. All the French newspapers talk of the 'liberalization of the regime.' Whereas, I believe that this is a fundamental misconception. The commentators who take this position are always surprised when we are witness to people who post *dazibao*[iii] being arrested, student or workers' demonstrations suppressed … Each time they write of 'a curb on liberalization.' But it is a nonsense. There never was any liberalization and the new political tendency has nothing to do with liberty. There is a transition from a system where revolutionary ideology held sway over technical efficiency to a system where the desire for technical growth effaces revolutionary ideology. The technical at any price and 'efficiency first' have nothing to do with liberalization.[6]

iii. Handwritten wall posters in large characters, expressing a political opinion; from 大 *dà* 'big', 字 *zì* 'character', and 報 *bào* 'newspaper or poster'. The posting of *dazibao* on public walls was a fundamental right under the Chinese constitution during the Mao era and the Democracy Wall period (1978–80); a right abrogated at Deng Xiaoping's initiative in 1980.

Writing in 1982, Ellul understood better than most political scientists or sinologists that technical advancement and capitalist economics did not imply progress towards political liberalization. In this he showed utmost clarity.[iv] However, he also foresaw a future China transforming its people into an 'advanced industrial proletariat' through industrialization and technology, which, he thought, might lead to a new revolution. Such a revolution has not, yet, occurred.

Ellul, whose writings did so much to inspire and foster the French and American ecology movements, saw it as inevitable that China would be obliged enthusiastically to engage in the technological system. He understood the dilemma of China's leadership but, surprisingly, seemed almost to welcome China's aggressive participation in the system. Perhaps he did so because of this belief that the resultant proletariat would represent a revolutionary potential to force the system to change. But that potential has not to date been realized; China's technological revolution has not led to political revolution or individual liberties.

Since, whatever humanity does to it, the planet itself will survive, the priority now is rather saving future generations, and thus Ellul's strategy is extremely pertinent to present-day China.[v] Ellul's 'road map of a possible future' demands

iv. I do not exclude myself from this misplaced optimism of the mid-80s: see Lee, *China's Lost Decade*, p. 134.

v. In 2015, I had the pleasure of hearing Professor Ignazio Musu of Ca' Foscari University give a talk entitled 'Towards a Green Economy'. Professor Musu, an economist, has devoted much of his recent career to ecological questions and the issue of sustainability. He has also visited China a number of times and encountered at first hand the contradictions between state directives aimed at improving environmental conditions and the state-driven imperatives focused on economic growth. Professor Musu talked about regulation, limits and the need to constrain growth, and the need for bottom-up civil society action to bring this recognizing the need for imposing ceilings and fixing limits. These ceilings—on pollution, on the depletion of resources—represent the 'boundaries which human action (and technology) must set so that life remains possible'. But their imposition is only a minimum requirement. As Ellul stresses, if humankind is interested in creating a new way of living, with more than just survival as its ambition, it will be necessary to go further, and fix 'limits that constitute the blueprint of a culture.'[7]

Yet, China's authorities, like rulers and indeed most of the ruled on the planet today, see technology as positive. Technology, and unfortunately that is almost all that remains of privately- and state-financed science, is not neutral. Science was never neutral. The very concept of 'objectivity' and 'neutrality' is part of what Castoriadis referred to in 1961 as the 'illusion of exact sciences as historical activity outside of history'. For as long as this illusion persists, the temptation will also exist to transpose 'techniques', 'methods' and 'categories' from the natural sciences to the 'historical sciences', and to human activity.[8] Science comes with a history. There is a historicity to the 'natural sciences', the 'exact sciences'. Science's ideology, and place in the imaginary of human society, has changed radically over the past 150 years: from science as truth in the mid-nineteenth century, to science as happiness in the 1920s and 1930s, to science as omnipotence in the postwar years, to science giving way to a technology that offers us eternal life.[9]

'The current ideology of science is an ideology of salvation.'[10] Not only do we see science as the only way forward, we

---

about. For that to be possible in China, a revolution in China's—and the rest of the world's—current culture would need to happen. That revolution would depend on a radical reassessment of the role and nature of science and technology in society and human activity. XV EAN Workshop, Venice, 14 May 2015.

also refuse to see its negative aspects. Science is the solution to all humanity's problems; this is particularly clear in health and medicine. Indeed, for Ellul, it is modern humanity's ostrich-like attitude that explains the failure thus far of the ecology movement fundamentally and radically to change our behaviour. China's overseas food footprint; the destruction of rainforests in order to create 'virtual water'—growing food on cleared land in Brazil to export back to China; the massive pollution of the oceans; the azureless skies of China's cities—these do not move us to act. The public feels an overwhelming sentiment of powerlessness when faced with gigantic threats, to the extent that we refuse to absorb negative information: leave it to science, it has all the answers. But science itself is not neutral, and China's integration into the world technologico-economic system has brought about repercussions that are not simply social and economic, but which have resulted in devastating consequences for the environment and climate of our planet.

Increasingly, studies on China, like this one, are no longer just about China—they are about the world. The realities we address today demand an intellectual capacity urgently to dismantle disciplinary and area studies boundaries. Unfortunately, transdisciplinarity, while often mooted in academic circles, has rarely been practised, and most academics remain resistant, if not downright inimical, to it. The particular problem of 'sinologists' or China specialists is not only that they have created their own object of study and observation, but that for over 100 years they have stood by and watched, and watched over, China (re) creating itself as the US. Sinologists often do not want to, or are ill-equipped to, question and observe themselves and their own societies. Yet now, after thirty years of so-called reforms that have turned China into first a productivist and then a consumerist society—thirty years that have seen China driven by a thirst for technology and everything else that constitutes the technological—we are unable to deny that, when we are looking at China, we are in fact looking at ourselves.

What goes for the world, what goes for humanity, goes for China too. But since President Xi came to power in 2012, China's authorities have propagated an image of China-as-dream. It is an image they have also tried to purvey to the world. And yet, China-as-dream already belongs to, and is integrated into, the wider universe-as-dream—a universe that Ellul understood as astutely as he did 1980s China:

> The universe we inhabit is becoming increasingly a dreamed universe, since the society of the spectacle is changing gradually into the society of the dream. This is brought about by the diffusion of spectacles of all sorts which we ask the spectator to internalize, but also brought about by the maintained dream of a science which immerses us into a world as yet unknown and incomprehensible.[11]

Here Ellul alludes to Guy Debord's critique of the society as a show society, or society of the spectacle: a consumer society in which power and politics have been assimilated to the strategies of communication, showbiz and advertising that were hitherto largely confined to the marketplace.[vi] Now, we must add the critique of omnipotent science and technology to this theory of 'the society of the spectacle'. In the late-twentieth-century world, Guy Debord noted the convergence of ways of exercising power in totalitarian societies with ways of exercising power in so-called liberal democracies, producing an 'integrated spectacle' (see Chapter 12); we are now confronted with a further element, which is the dreamed universe.

vi. Ellul and Debord respected each other's work and had met and corresponded. They met in Paris in 1962 (see Debord, *Correspondance*, vol. II, p. 177), and corresponded in 1968 (Debord, *Correspondance*, vol. III, p. 269).

Spectacular society has not been transcended; it has mutated. The convergence perceived by Debord in 1988 did indeed occur in the decades that followed his analysis. Ideologies seemed to melt away with the twilight of the twentieth century, but in fact disguised themselves as other dreams. The New World Order of a post-Communist era appeared to have dawned, one of universal happiness made possible by technology and paid for by capitalism; the American ideology seemed to have won. But that dream was of short duration. It was broken by the awakening of petty, retrograde, xenophobic, nationalist, and fundamentalist dreams, made possible by yet another crisis of capitalism and constructed on the ruins of a (post)colonial world order's logic.

At the beginning of the twenty-first century, we still inhabited a world of seemingly different imaginaries and projected dreams; dreams as both individual and collective projects. But more than ever these dreams were articulated and sustained through an assemblage of spectacles that did not seek to hide widespread human misery and environmental catastrophe on a planetary scale, but rather to mediate them by integrating them into the show of the everyday; witness the migration crisis caused by years of bombing of Syria after the government crackdown that followed the 2011 Arab Spring.

In the twenty-first century, we have been called on to live a dream not of our own imagining. It is a dream in which words are no longer needed to stimulate the imagination, a dream whose images are provided ready-made, and which is articulated by an array of technological gadgets, electronic entertainments, and mediated fears and hopes. This has been the moment of the 'oneiro-spectacular society': the society of the spectacle of dreams.

14

XI'S 'CHINA DREAM', TECHNOLOGICAL NIGHTMARE AND 'HOODLUM DIPLOMACY'

From the turn of the twenty-first century onwards, China's economic power grew massively, and with it a desire to create, control and disseminate its cultural image abroad. This gave rise to a cultural diplomatic offensive to displace long-standing foreign discourses on and about China with a cultural imaginary and historical narrative generated by the Chinese authorities themselves. But at the same time, in China itself, there was contestation of the authorities' control over society through daily strikes and social unrest. In the cultural sphere, resistance came from the likes of avant-garde artist Ai Weiwei, who, before being allowed to leave China, was under house arrest.[i]

As we have seen, after the Tiananmen Massacre in 1989—now out of living memory for some 40 per cent of the country's current population—China's authorities vigorously advanced the country's integration into the world technologico-economic system, gaining membership of its major organizations of

i. Ai Weiwei must battle constantly against the global show of which he is now a part, and which empowers his art to make such an impact. His contestation, which is sincere enough, is also useful to Western critics of China, but hardly ever provokes them into concrete action. See Ai Weiwei's film on the global refugee crisis, *Human Flow* (2017).

economic and political power, modernizing the military, preparing to put a person on the moon, and joining the club of nations engaged in the 'war on terror'. Yet despite these aspirations to global 'normality', the government did not manage to control and suppress dissent, and despite all its efforts the Chinese culture that the world most appreciates is not that which is promoted and sponsored by the state, but that which is unofficial and fractious. Ai Weiwei has done more to alert the world to the fact that there are really existing creative and concerned Chinese than all the Confucius Institutes the authorities have launched around the world. When Ai focuses on non-Chinese subjects, he does great service to those he is directly concerned about—disaster victims, refugees, the excluded—but also foregrounds, and distances himself from, the obsession of the modern Chinese intellectual and artist: China itself, an obsession that has existed for a hundred years or more.[ii]

Ai Weiwei has stood out against particularism, seen the global, common, human interest in the world's current crises, and demonstrated an understanding of the terrain on which any artist, actor or agent ought to stand. It is not about the object—it is even beyond our relationship with the 'object'—it is about questioning ourselves.[1] Commenting on his film *Human Flow*, he said: 'The refugee crisis is not about refugees, rather, it is about us.' He continued:

ii. As mentioned in Chapter 4, the 'obsession' with China was first identified and discussed by the exiled Chinese academic C. T. Hsia, in his widely-read yet controversial essay 'Obsession with China: the moral burden of modern Chinese literature'. While writers in the 4 May tradition adopted a critical political stance and were in tune with contemporary social contestation, they were according to Hsia highly inward-looking, with a tendency to see 'the conditions of China as peculiarly Chinese and not applicable elsewhere'. It is a tendency that Ai Weiwei has eschewed, as did his father the poet Ai Qing before him. For more on Ai Qing see Lee, *China's Lost Decade*, pp. 34–68.

> Establishing the understanding that we all belong to one humanity is the most essential step for how we might continue to coexist on this sphere we call Earth ... There are many borders to dismantle, but the most important are the ones within our own hearts and minds—these are the borders that are dividing humanity from itself.[2]

In other words, the focus in a globalized system can no longer be merely on one's own backyard, because feeding a country is to the detriment of not just another country, but of the planet's common resources; because today's comfortable urban dweller is tomorrow's refugee; because the pollution that rains down rains down on us all.

Within China, dissident voices erupt from time to time, and continue to be silenced by the authorities. In 2014, the central authorities condemned to long prison sentences a number of academics, the most well-known of whom was the Chinese Uighur economist Ilham Tohti. Professor Tohti regularly spoke out to defend the rights of the Uighur minority in Xinjiang and to question the central administration's policy in this region, but he had never advocated violence, nor the cause of separatism of which he was accused; his criticisms and propositions were based on his academic research, which had been carried out with the utmost rigour.[3] On a larger scale, in what became known as the 'Umbrella Movement' of 2014, the people of Hong Kong demonstrated en masse their unwillingness to accept the undemocratic future being foisted upon them.

Under the terms of the 1984 Sino-British Joint Declaration, agreed between the PRC and the territory's former colonial power, Hong Kong is theoretically guaranteed a 'high degree of autonomy'. The state has reacted to rising political opposition with a crackdown on those Hong Kongers demanding the rights they were promised, and which the Umbrella Revolution sought to defend as the financial district was occupied by protesters. The following year saw the spectacular abduction to mainland China of a group of Hong Kong-based publishers; one of them, Gui Minhai, was a Swedish national, seized by agents of the Chinese state while he was in Thailand.[iii/4] During the night of 8–9 February 2016, in what became known as the 'Fishball Revolution', Hong Kong youth vigorously defended street-hawkers' time-honoured practice of selling fish balls in the working-class Mong Kok district during the New Year festivities. Police insensitivity had sparked off welling frustration against the authorities, and protesters and riot police spent the night battling in Hong Kong's streets—scenes not seen since the anti-British riots of 1967. In 2017, elected legislators were barred from taking up their seats for refusing to take the oath of allegiance to the PRC authorities, and in early 2018 candidates were disqualified from standing for office because their party, Demosisto, advocated self-determination for Hong Kong.[iv]

In the same period, mainland China has witnessed the continuous harassment and arrests of Chinese human rights activists, the expulsion of foreign NGO workers and journalists who dared to shed light on rights issues, and a continued governmental disregard for the political and economic rights of

iii. The five men—Gui Minhai 桂民海, Lui Por 呂波, Cheung Chi-ping 張志平, Lee Po 李波, and Lam Wing-Kee 林榮基—who would spend eight months in solitary confinement, were all associated with Causeway Bay Books and its publishing arm Mighty Current Media, located on Hong Kong island. The company was set to publish a book about President Xi Jinping. The men went missing between October and November 2015. In January 2018, Gui Minhai was rearrested on a train in mainland China while accompanied by Swedish diplomats; he subsequently appeared on Chinese television to say that he was voluntarily helping the police with their inquiries.

iv. In the coastal city of Lianyungang 連雲港, about 500 km (310 miles) north of Shanghai. See Reischer, 'Protests threaten China's nuclear energy plans'.

Uighurs and Tibetans. Occasionally, as in mid-2016, when Chinese citizens protested en masse against the construction of a French nuclear waste recycling plant near Shanghai, dissent cannot be crushed so easily.[v]

All of this contestation contrasted starkly with President Xi Jinping's heralded pursuit of the consumerist 'Chinese Dream', again redolent of 1950s Americanization, which aimed to curry favour with China's rising middle class. The 'Dream', which is largely economic, also involves seducing global partners such as the United Kingdom, which hosted a state visit for President Xi in late 2015 amidst the fanfare of a China–UK 'Golden Partnership'.[5] Moreover, China's authorities have invested massively abroad in the context of the 'New Silk Road' or 'Belt and Road', whereby 'Beijing has pledged more money than went into the postwar Marshall plan on high-speed rail schemes around the world in an effort to secure diplomatic allies and develop new markets.'[6]

The initial period of President Xi's mandate can be described as having had a dreamlike quality, in the sense that, economically, a significant nouveau riche middle class was still partially satisfied with the materialism of the Chinese Dream. However, no capitalist economy is ever immune from inherent,

v. Already involved (in partnership with the French EDF) in financing and constructing the UK's Hinkley Point nuclear power plant, China's nuclear industry set about building a plant in Poland (*The China Daily*, 'CGN in talk to build first nuclear power plant in Poland', 25 July 2017, http://www.chinadaily.com.cn/business/2017-07/25/content_30241352.htm, last accessed 19 August 2017). Meanwhile, 'China's Exim Bank is bankrolling 82 per cent of the cost of Pakistan's new reactors and is thought to be contributing to the construction of reactors in Romania alongside the Industrial and Commercial Bank of China'. Matthew Cottee, 'China's nuclear export ambitions run into friction', *Financial Times*, 2 August 2017, https://www.ft.com/content/84c25750-75da-11e7-90c0-90a9d1bc9691 (last accessed 10 July 2018).

systemic crisis and huge segments of China's population now realize there is no future for them in this dreamscape. Moreover, the Chinese state has increasingly and openly showed its totalitarian claws both domestically and abroad. At home, never have civil rights been so disrespected since the post-Tiananmen backlash as they have been under Xi Jinping's reign, and in its foreign relations China's administration has become increasingly bellicose; witness its increasing presence in the South China Sea.

For hundreds of millions, then, the Chinese Dream has turned to 'nightmare'. In a flouting of the most minimal respect for the rule of law, individuals are picked off, abducted, and made to recant. In Renaissance Europe, nightmares were associated with the myth of a fiend, called the 'leaper', the 'throttler', or the 'Incubus', from the Latin *inculare*, 'to lie down on'. The fiend would lie on its victims in their sleep and suffocate them.[7] Indeed, Xi's China rather resembles the embryonic England of Kazuo Ishiguro's *The Buried Giant*, in which the long-deceased Merlin has cast a spell on a dragon so that it will breathe over the land a mist destroying the inhabitants' capacity to remember, thus rendering them ignorant and credulous. In twenty-first-century China, a whole generation no longer knows or believes the Tiananmen Massacre actually happened.

'In order to dream, you must first be asleep.'[vi] More than ever before, the now technologically-equipped Chinese state behaves like a twenty-first-century Incubus as it envelops its citizens, who have been induced into a dream-like sleep, stifled with somniferous propaganda, consumer goods and the promise of a brighter future. Indeed, in the space of a few short years, Xi's spectacular-dream society has morphed from the

vi. A comment made to me in China in May 2018 by a young professional woman responding to a question about Xi Jinping's 'China dream' (*Zhongguo meng* 中國夢).

promised dream into a tightly controlled, technology-intensive, nightmare society, what we might term the Society of the Spectacular Incubus, in which regnant power smothers the populace with electronic surveillance, violently throttles dissenters, and pursues a policy of aggressive undiplomacy towards its international neighbours.

With Xi Jinping Thought enshrined in the constitution of the Communist Party of China, and his effectively being made president-for-life by a March 2018 state constitutional amendment, the situation seems unlikely to improve in the near future, despite the wishful thinking of the West's China-watchers. As Ellul reminded us as far back as the 1980s, there 'never was any liberalization and the new political tendency has nothing to do with liberty.'[8] What is more, were the buried giant monster ever to be slain, what might follow is less than certain.

In 1968, Debord wrote of the 'spectacle' as 'the diplomatic representation of hierarchic society to itself, where all other expression is banned', and observed that 'the most modern is also the most archaic.'[9] In the second decade of the twenty-first century, 'diplomatic representation' has become most undiplomatic. A new form of political show is now widespread. It involves a set of practices that are common currency not only in China, but also in Russia and Turkey. The conduct of these countries' foreign policies has become no more than a virulent form of 'hoodlum diplomacy', and the power that is meant to counter such behaviour, the United States, has been under Donald Trump's administration little better.[10]

The dream-spectacle phase of global politics started to disintegrate barely twenty years after George Bush Senior's declaration of a 'new world order'. In Europe and America, increasing popular disillusionment expressed itself in forms of nationalistic identitarian politics; in re-emergent racist and anti-immigrant ideologies; in neofascist and populist political parties gaining electoral ground; in the disastrous consequences of Western-engineered upheaval in Libya, Iraq, Iran, Afghanistan and Syria, resulting in a migration crisis unparalleled since World War II; and in 'home-grown' Islamist jihadists engaging in terror in the West. The enchantment of the dream has been seriously undermined in the popular imagination.

The dream-turned-nightmare of the technical, the technological and the economic now serves only the aggrandizement of the state and its ambitions of political and territorial expansion, whether in the South China Sea or on the Ukrainian borderlands. The spectacle of dreams has mutated systemically into an unmediated show of fear: the society of the spectacular Incubus. The systemic demon that tyrannizes and subjugates—the seductive and phoney harmony of the first decade of the twenty-first century, the long-cherished and nourished simulacrum of normality—has spawned a nightmare society of 'enriched privation', marked by technologically-maintained insecurity, fear and brutality. As Debord might have said, the spectacular poverty of those societies in which the convergence of totalitarianism with the technologico-economic system prevails now presents itself as an immense accumulation of nightmares.

15

TOWARDS A CONCLUSION

Was what is now happening in China and the world avoidable? Perhaps, but only if other choices could had been made sixty, 100, or even 150 years ago. What we witness now is the ultimate product of the (post)colonial, nationalist road to 'salvation' to which the logic of Versailles gave rise. But the inevitability of China's and Japan's enclosure in this logic was already embedded in the imaginary of their intellectual elites by the late nineteenth and early twentieth centuries. The roadmap to today's China was crystallized in Chen Duxiu's 1919 slogan of 'Mr Science and Mr Democracy'. Mr Democracy never reared his head, except perhaps in a confused way in the 1980s, and democracy or no, the technologico-economic outcome would doubtless have been the same.[i]

China's failure to realize the half of Chen Duxiu's slogan that demanded 'Democracy' is in part explained by the success of the other half, 'Science'. Science has never needed democracy

i. Let us also recall that what happened first in Japan and then in China and the territorially colonized world—the reorganization of knowledge, the epistemological revolutions, the denigration of local knowledges, or what E. P. Thompson called 'common sense'—had also occurred earlier in the West. There it had resulted in the kind of cultural impoverishment, human upheaval, alienation and misery we now see among China's recently urbanized new proletariat.

to flourish. The one was not predicated upon the other; the failure of the post-Communist world to shed totalitarian ways has demonstrated as much. Science in any case has always been fundamentally 'colonialist'. As Vandana Singh has written, science 'is so flawed in the sense that it is so easily appropriated by powerful forces, such as colonialism. There is a link between science and colonialism that cannot be denied.'[1]

But while science and technology may not need freedom to advance, and perhaps thrive without it, cultural creativity craves it. While China's leaders have implemented the integration of the Western technologico-economic model, the officially promoted arts and culture have clearly failed to impress beyond China's borders. Since the beginning of the twentieth century, hegemonic cultural production has favoured and represented the reinvention of an industrialized technological power, of the march towards sovereignty through emulation of Western modernity.

We may even go so far as to say that the official literature and culture of the PRC era has functioned as an instrument of the postcolonial poisoned chalice, insofar as it has shaped, negotiated and represented the post-Versailles ideology that has led to China's transformation into a major agent of the world technologico-economic system. And yet, beneath that dominant cultural production, there has always existed a current engaging in a critique of that system. When, as has often been the case during most of the twentieth and twenty-first centuries, cultural creativity has been suppressed and censored, this has resulted in a reactive, critical, dissident culture—for, as surely as night follows day, where there is oppression and censorship there will be resistance and dissent.

Rather than imitate and laud the technologico-economic system, unofficial modern Chinese creativity has drawn on the West's, and twentieth-century China's own, critical traditions to create not an alternative modernity, but a cultural modernism of contestation. This parallel creativity in poetry, fiction, film and artistic practice is at odds with the spectacular vision that is the official Chinese Dream. This disjuncture explains why China's recent cultural diplomatic policy initiatives have failed, and why Western and other Asian visions of the dreamed universe remain hegemonic. Official American, French, German, British, Spanish, and other cultural diplomacies are supported by a spectacularly enchanted universe; they constitute a modern global dream represented by Hollywood, Disney, the Cannes Festival, singers, and film and sports stars. These cultures offer an exotic reverie to the consumer often foregrounding the new and innovative, the culturally vibrant and cosmopolitan. The power of Asian, non-state-driven cultural diplomacy has also been extremely powerful in this respect: Japanese manga and video games, Korean TV series and K-Pop, Indian cinema, and Thai cinema are among the most spectacular examples.

China has given the world a cultural diplomatic initiative named after Confucius, a name that symbolizes a millenary order, stability and obedience; an ideology that the very founders of the modern Chinese state had railed against at the turn of the twentieth century. This strategy of promoting as Chinese something exotic that is backward-looking and out of step with today's realities, and which excludes its most influential living artists and creative talent, means that this soft-diplomatic policy is not only ineffective—it is truly counter-productive.

There persists an idea that there has been, or can be, a 'Chinese modernity'—one that can be different if it reinvents itself within an identitarian cultural capsule; if it 'reserves' itself a 'Chinese' cultural space, and so models itself on the heralded Japanese example of a supposedly particular modernity. To propose this is really to misunderstand the nature of the historical processes that have unfolded since the nineteenth century, and to misunderstand the reality of the dangers facing humanity. The 2011 disaster at Fukushima was not a problem of a specifically Japanese modernity, but of a global industrial modernity in which technology had been left the upper, indeed the only, hand.

It is as if there were a psychosocial schizophrenia that has gripped China's authorities. On the one hand, they invest in and promote a Western technologico-economic model, while on the other they implement a culturally conservative policy aimed at producing a hermetic cultural and academic system to constrain 'Westernness' to the technical sphere. In the impossibility of this political balancing act lies a first element of hope. The second lies in the problematic nature of the system itself. If there is a way out of this limitless model into which nineteenth-century and twentieth-century colonialism has led the world, it is in its inherent faultiness.

We see in today's China the imperfections and misfirings of the system: the high-speed trains that derail for lack of respect for security provisions; buildings and bridges that collapse because built by non-qualified personnel or because the concrete has been watered down; roads that crumble because of being laid onto cardboard; cruise ships that capsize because warning signs are ignored; and the constant damage to public health caused by the toxic pollution of air, water and land.[2] There are further obstacles and curbs on the system: the inability of institutions to move forward at the same speed as technological developments, and the widespread social contestation of labour.

Once again, nothing can be changed on a planetary scale without China's participation. If humanity is to step back from the abyss, then China must do so first. In large part, it falls to China—colonized by, and yet currently also the agent of, the technologico-economic system—to create a new culture. The first step would be the setting of 'willed-for limits'. The unlimited is incapable of founding and constituting a new culture, or a person: 'It is by establishing limits that humans institute themselves as human.'[3] Without China's active co-operation, even were the rest of the world to opt for the path of ungrowth, the nightmare would continue. The forty-plus Chinese nuclear power reactors in operation in 2018, the score of power plants under construction, and those about to start construction, present not only a mortal danger for China's people but for China's neighbours also.[ii/4]

If China's people wish to create a different future, if they wish to benefit from a decent quality of life and not simply to survive, then they will have not only to fix limits, but to think about how to live differently. Such an effort would constitute a response, albeit belated, to the 'progress' proffered by the global system that has travelled from imperialism, to modernization, to globalization. This future course is not impossible. Once again, what has occurred in the West will occur, and is already occurring, in China: a shift in opinion towards 'disappointment, fear, and questioning', a 'widespread revolt of workers against efficiency and the subordination of labour to yield.'[5] There are demonstrations and minor rebellions against the system on a daily basis; at the individual level, suicides in the face of the inhumane working conditions of those known as 'iSlaves' are common.[6] It is at this price that the world's

ii. The author was reminded of our narrowly nationalistic vision of nuclear power, and of the illusion of unilaterally stepping back from dependence on nuclear technology, during a 2014 workshop on the Fukushima disaster, when a Japanese speaker suggested that Japanese civil society was now willing and ready to push for the elimination of nuclear power plants in Japan. However, Chinese civil society on the other side of the East China Sea not being able to follow suit, how safe can that leave Japan, not to mention China, and to what extent can nuclear energy be a mere national question?

consumers are furnished with the electronic trinkets and playthings that fill their enchanted dreamscapes.[iii]

The rise of productivist and now consumerist China has not only revived and prolonged capitalism for a certain period of time; it has also permitted the expansion of the technological system it feeds. At the same time, China's participation in this system brings nearer the inevitable social and environmental crisis that Ellul predicted in the 1980s. Now that China's leadership have fully integrated the country into a system riddled with faults and cracks, Ellul's 1986 analysis resonates even louder and truer.

China's contribution to the world's future well-being does not lie in reimagining for itself an alternative cultural modernity, nor in marketing a cultural diplomacy dream palace, but rather in contributing to a global conversation focused on limits. Only then will the real issues facing the world's present and future populations be frontally addressed. Only then will the mystique and myth of growth be interrogated and undermined, and only then will creativity, *poïesis*, reassert its centrality to human society. Again, I use the word creativity in the sense employed by Castoriadis. *Poïesis* is the activity of the artisan and the artist that is not subordinated to the constraints of subsistence. It is creation. This creativity will entail new forms of culture, but it will certainly imply a new poetry, or *poïesis*, of daily life. It will necessitate abandoning the dreamed universe, jettisoning the handle of the barrel-organ, and creating a new organic melody. Only then will the sense of *techne* as human capacity to make and perform be restored.

iii. The 2014 suicide of the Apple supplier Foxconn's worker-poet Xu Lizhi 许立志 was alas not a rare occurrence. Xu had 'migrated' from rural China to Shenzhen to find work and dreamed of being a librarian or working in a bookshop. His poetry draws on his experience of the everyday life and harsh working and living conditions of a factory worker.

But, if we are to attempt change in the sense of 'ungrowth', abandonment of current economic dogma, and the restoration of the ecological balance of our physical environment, then this strategy would need rapid implementation. A new music, a new imaginary, a new ideology in the best sense of the term, together with propitious intellectual and moral conditions, would be indispensable to the creation of a new human spirit. Specifically, narrow self-interest would need to be overcome, and a collectively shared frugality and 'revolutionary austerity' instituted, based on common consent. All in all, it would demand a profound political and cultural shake-up, and a shared and global awakening from our collective dream. This could only be rendered possible by a 'cultural revolution' and the institution of 'an ethics of powerlessness'.[7] Alluding to the doctrines espoused by Gandhi and the civil rights movement, Ellul described the spirit of 'powerlessness' as going beyond non-violence, as constituting 'the choice ... not to dominate, not to exploit, and even not to use the means of power that could be available to us.'[8] Ellul's proposition would not sound unfamiliar to those familiar with the philosophers we call Taoists, Zhuangzi and Laozi, who espoused similar strategies in China-Before-China two millennia ago.

16

CODA

I should like to end this book with a reflection on the place of China, and of what we imagine to be 'Chinese' things and thoughts, in how we might imagine a common future for humanity.

There has been much excitement in recent years around the idea of a new geological age brought about by the influence of humankind on the planet. Some place the start of this new age in the 1950s and the beginning of the impact of mass consumer society. Today, for instance, plastics have found their way into the sediment which will form tomorrow's rocks; our impact on global warming is also a recent phenomenon. Others push the start of this new age back to the start of the Industrial Revolution in the eighteenth century. However, the impact of humankind on fauna, flora and the very fabric of the Earth stretches much further back, to the vast migration that took place around 60,000 years ago when we all came out of what is now called Africa. It was then that we colonized lands previously solely occupied by non-humanoid animals; it was then that we started to kill off big beasts. Subsequently we started to settle and engage in agriculture and thus establish our domination over land and water.[i]

i. I am indebted to the environmental ethicist, J. Baird Callicott, for

Records of humankind's reflection on how to limit its impact on 'Nature' go back to early philosophers, by which I mean both those we now call 'Greek', and those we now call 'Chinese'. And it is precisely because we now recognize our impact as more than simply a modern problem that such philosophical texts are useful in reflecting on a future for mankind on a now totalized, globalized planet. Plato has been long recognized as part of common human heritage; so too are the Taoist philosophers Zhuangzi, Laozi and Liezi. If I cite them here, it is not because—as many of today's Chinese commentators would have it—they are philosophers of the 'Chinese nation' (*Zhonghua minzu* 中华民族), but because they did their philosophy at a moment when they took themselves to be thinking for the known world; a time when Plato was ignorant of Zhuangzi, and Zhuangzi was ignorant of Plato.

Today we know of the existence of both; we have no excuse for not taking into consideration the thought of Zhuangzi, just as Chinese people today read Plato. They are both the world's philosophers. Both talked about limits to humankind's exploitation of Nature. It was an incomplete Nature, for Zhuangzi in particular, for this was the *tianxia* 天下: 'under-the-heavens', the 'world'—warped by Confucius into a polity to be governed by a supreme monarch, and subsequently mistranslated into English as 'Empire'. For Zhuangzi, humankind had subtracted itself from 'Nature', from the 'under-the-heavens', and now sought, as did Confucius, to treat what remained as an external object to be mastered and exploited.

Throughout this book, I have referred to two modern thinkers, Ellul and Castoriadis, whom I regard as essential

---

conversations I had with him during the conference 'Representing Nature in the Age of the Anthropocene', 22–23 March 2018, at the Institut d'Etudes Transtextuelles et Transculturelles (IETT), Lyon.

contributors to the debate on the future of humankind and our planet. It is the absence of limits that has led to the current environmental and climatic crisis, and any hope for the world's future resides in fixing some—in the discussion on limits, what Ellul and Castoriadis have to say is invaluable. The consequences of this lack of limits are to be seen in what we have taken to calling the Anthropocene, conceived as a recent period in world history. By 'world' I mean not simply the physical and biological environment, but the 'Nature' that was regretted by the philosophers more than 2,000 years ago; a Nature in which humankind had been an integral part, the *phusis* before our separation from it—what the Taoists called the 'myriad things', the Universe.

The Taoists hoped to invert the trend, to repair the damage done by this separation which already in their time was all around them: in agriculture, in the towns, in large-scale public works, all representing an ambition to dominate Nature. Early in the twentieth century, Jacques Ellul and his colleague Bernard Charbonneau had identified the deleterious impact of the disregard for limits as a central question of our time.[ii] By 1935, they had already identified 'unlimited production' as a core question of modernity:

> the decisive fact about modernity: the technical had led to the triumph of instrumental reason. The technical is much more than a set of industrial processes, it is a 'general procedure', that is to say an imaginary of practices focussed on unlimited production, efficiency and the multiplication of abstract and oppressive systems. Plunged into an environment consisting solely of means, totally mediatized, and thus with no control over his environment, *homo technologicus* is confronted by a universe where all seems

ii. Bernard Charbonneau (1910–96) was, and remains, a major inspiration to the French ecology movement.

> fated, and is baffled by its scale (whether in the domains of economics, media, industry, or work).[1]

Charbonneau and Ellul questioned the presumption that the technological and the technical were neutral. By the technical, Ellul intended not simply technology, but the technical procedures present in modernity, for the technical 'engenders the development of power' and, far from leading to emancipation, 'power engenders imbalances and becomes uncontrollable, for it inevitably encourages specialization and immensity'.[2]

Writing in 1977, at a moment when China had just emerged from the Cultural Revolution and two decades before China was to become a major vehicle of 'over-production', Ellul, already talking of the minimum limits necessary for humanity's survival, insisted on the distinction between 'thresholds' (*seuils*) and 'limits' (*limites*):

> Thresholds represent the boundaries between which the action of humankind (and of the technical) must be situated for survival to remain possible. It is a question of necessity. And when we talk of nuisances, pollution, the exhaustion of natural resources, we configure threshold levels … It is thus just a question of conditions necessary for survival. But this means nothing in terms of the creation of a civilization, of a culture: here humankind must fix its own limits which constitute the blueprint of a culture … 'Zero growth' is by no means the guarantee that a new culture will emerge, it simply provides the possibility for one … Contrary to what we believe, it is the fixing of limits which creates freedom … I believe nothing is so fundamental as this question of willed-for limits.[3]

For Castoriadis, these voluntary, willed-for, embraced limits (*limites volontaires*) are the only valid ones:

> The only veritable limitation that democracy can entail is self-limitation, which in the final analysis, can only be the work of

> individuals (of citizens) educated by and for democracy ... This amounts to saying that democracy, just like philosophy, necessarily rejects the sacred ... it demands that human beings accept in their real behaviour what they have almost never wished truly to accept ... that they are mortal.[4]

Castoriadis is not talking about each individual taking their bottles to the bottle-bank; what he means is that each individual should take responsibility, and militate, for limits that will have an impact on their own everyday behaviour, and that these limits need to be decided and put in place democratically. This raises a huge question for China. Unless subscribing to the view that a totalitarian state has greater powers to make its people observe limits, and that such is a good thing for the climate control agenda, the situation of China's population gives cause for extreme concern. In a country where demanding that food safety standards be respected or that independent air pollution statistics be published may be construed as dissidence, how are China's citizens to make an impact on the conditions that are making their lives shorter and more disagreeable? Here again, the central question is that of democracy, or rather its absence.

Later on, in 1990, Castoriadis would return to the themes of limits and of 'cohabitation', or living together, with Nature. And in this call for cohabitation, we may hear echoes of earlier enlightened philosophers, whom we now call Greek or Chinese, who were faced with the reality that was humankind's separation from the remainder of Nature, the rupture effected by humankind's self-subtraction from the world, its rhythms and its practices. This was a Nature in which humankind had previously participated in mythic times. Given this reality, the most the philosophers could suggest was a convergence of humankind and the rest of Nature, and ideas of how to manage humanity's impact on it.

By the time of Plato, there was already a reflection in Athens on the question of *homo consumens*, the dynamics of *thumos* (consumption), and how such consumption could be moderated through education to ensure the survival of the *polis*, both as a place and as a body of citizens.[5] Five thousand miles away, other philosophers were also recommending a 'co-habitation', a convergence, advancing the formula *tian ren he yi* 天人合一, which translates literally as 'heaven—humankind—come together—as one', where 'heaven' is the natural world. This formula recognized that the ideal condition of humanity as an integral part of this world was long gone, and that separation and alienation had become the rule. It was, if anything, a longing to patch things up. In the twentieth century Castoriadis would declare: 'A change of attitude is indispensable. We must rid ourselves of our fantasies of domination and unlimited expansion, stop limitless exploitation of our planet, lovingly live together with it, like an English gardener.'[6]

A fine sentiment, though one that ignores that the English garden is refined and groomed, very structured, and bursting with pesticides. But let us allow Castoriadis his idealized garden. What it represents is clear: the 'cohabitation' is humankind caring for the garden, looking after the garden rather than letting it be. Of course, in Taoism's ideal Nature, there would be no garden at all. Such a garden will always be the result of humankind's attempt to structure Nature, the object of the gardener's attempts to master it, even when doing so lovingly. The garden will always be found on the other side of a rupture: that separating humankind from Nature. Perhaps as in the Greek *polis* so precious to Castoriadis, it was for him a question of pragmatism, of what might be possible now—an unpaved garden, while not a paradise, would always be preferable to a 'parking lot'. Once again, the question for Castoriadis is that of self-limitation and specifically of 'self-limited freedom':

> Autonomy, freedom, is not just the abolition of external constraints or psychological urges; it is also the establishment of a different kind of relationship between our deep-seated urges, whether individual or collective, and decision-making bodies able to select between them, to give them form or to prevent them from emerging into reality. It is the role of a thinking and deliberating subjectivity at the level of the individual, of democratic institutions in the collective arena, since democracy is the regime of collective reflexion and of self-limited freedom.[7]

But, as Chinese environmental and human rights activists might retort, before one's freedoms are limited, either individually or collectively, they must already exist. In the China of Xi Jinping, there is no 'collective reflexion' on limits; only an autocratic imposition of ready-made decisions. Here it would be an appropriate point to return to the Taoist philosophers, because what is implied in Castoriadis's approach is the limitation of both power and desire, a question that was central to Taoism.[iii]

The Taoism to which I refer is not to be confused with mysticism. It is rather a body of reflections based on observation that nowadays we might refer to as 'scientific'; just as Plato was interested in measurement and appearance, so the texts attributed to Zhuangzi are much concerned with the relative size of objects and the question of perspective. Neither is the Taoism I refer to a religion; the popular religion called Taoism is a much later phenomenon. What I intend by Taoism is a

iii. Once again, I have to reject the label 'Chinese' philosophers, since at the time of the first Taoists, 2,000–2,500 years ago, there was no China, neither in reality nor in the imagination of those who inhabited the lands constituting what we moderns ache to call 'Ancient China'. Let us recall that those who have left us these philosophical texts lived in distinct, often geographically distant states, spoke in different dialects, and practised a language, or languages, totally different from the one used today in the China of Xi Jinping.

philosophy. It is not a 'wisdom', but a reflection which is often political and always philosophical. Neither do Taoist texts favour a simple rejection of power and its exercise; rather, they stand as a critical reflection upon political practice.

However, the world of the Taoists was also the world of Confucius, who developed and propagated a philosophy of governance. Indeed, it was more an ideology concerned with the practice of power, than a philosophy. At about the time that writings attributed to Confucius were being collated, the first five books of what would become the Bible were taking form. Interestingly, Ellul has a thesis as to how the history recounted by the Bible is intimately connected with the march towards urban civilization, with the ultimate destination that was the city. Everything starts in the Garden of Eden and moves towards the utopia of Jerusalem.[8] As in William Blake's 1804 poem 'And did those feet in ancient time', the ambition is not to preserve Nature, but to build Jerusalem in it. Paradise is the city built out of, and against, 'England's green and pleasant land'. Likewise, Confucius's ideology followed a similar logic. The physical environment was there to be dominated and utilized to construct the perfect world—a world deemed to have existed in a halcyon, bygone age, yet nevertheless located in an urban civilization, contained within city walls, and at a remove from the savage countryside and its inhabitants. For Confucius, the world was a political entity needing to be structured and ordered. What mattered was governance, superficial rules, obedience to the rites—that is to say, to the varnish, the urbane. However, for the Taoists, or at least for the texts that are associated with them, Confucius propagated a thought that was anathema. Confucian rules of conduct represented the mere vestiges of lip-service to a morality that had been reduced from something akin to a universal moral force, in order to set rules of etiquette.

For Zhuangzi, the world that would ideally be re-established was not the mythical kingdom of wise kings, but that moment before civilization and the dominance of the urban; before humankind's separation from a now externalized world. What mattered to Zhuangzi and the other Taoists was not meddling in the petty politics of the various courts vying for power, but how power was to be exercised and limited. The common misconception that Zhuangzi avoids taking a position vis-à-vis power and those who exercise it is entirely false. But it is an idea propagated by the later commentaries, which have been systematically, unreflectingly recycled by Western sinologists.[9]

As demonstrated by Jean François Billeter, 'rather than a rejection of power, Zhuangzi displays a radical critique of power'.[10] It was one of the later philosophical commentators—the ideological spin-doctors of their age—who reduced the Taoist philosophy to the level of small beer in the syncretic panoply of philosophical texts making up the ideology that would maintain in power a succession of monarchs and dynasties following unification, rationalization and centralization of the states of China-Before-China. Guo Xiang 'transformed a scathing critique of power into an apology for an abdication of power and for moral difference. In emasculating the *Zhuangzi* [the text] he ensured its enduring place in the culture of the dominant classes.'[11] In other words, by watering down and reinterpreting Zhuangzi's critique of power, it was rendered a harmless adjunct to the mainstream Confucian-dominated ideology.

However, if we restore the original, critical bite to the *Zhuangzi*, it enables us to think once again about willed-for, voluntary limits, since Zhuangzi tells us that 'humans wear away their energy and ask for disaster because they are the playthings of their own desire.'[12] The 'power' referred to by Zhuangzi is a moral strength, the fortitude to master the will-to-do. Zhuangzi believes that we can acquire the power both 'to want not' and 'not to want', and thus to avoid doing the wrong thing.[13] As for Ellul, he writes of *non-puissance*: not impotence, but a conscious decision not to exercise our power—to limit ourselves, as those who govern us have done, by some secular miracle, in their non-use of nuclear arms. Zhuangzi too had referred to this non-exercise of power that operates through a mastery of the will. However, in the twenty-first century, we are not all equal in the exercise or non-exercise of will. Those who live on atolls about to be submerged may have the will, but do not have the power. Those Chinese who agitate for environmental rights and against local governments flouting health and safety laws or environmental regulations are in no position to demand, let alone enforce, the limits that China collectively needs to impose.

However, the 'guilty party' is nowadays not an ogre. It is not Xi Jinping, nor is it one of the other 'strong men' who dominate the world's large countries; neither is it the ruling class, nor is it a wicked country. As Ellul put it, as long ago as 1966, we are 'all engaged in a process of common evolution' in which the world has become one, in the way it works and it the way it expresses itself. This oneness goes well beyond all other divisions, whether of class or nation.[14]

As we have seen, the China at which we point the finger when we talk of climate change, pollution of earth, sea and air, or the exhaustion of natural resources at home and abroad is no more or less responsible than others for the state of the planet. China may currently be turning the handle of the world's technology-driven economy, but it cannot decide in isolation to stop doing so. Such an outcome can only be the result of a collective act of will to fix the necessary limits. If Castoriadis is to be believed, and the only valid kind of limit-fixing is one accepted and promulgated democratically—how can we in the West accept anything less without condoning totalitarianism?—then there remains a long march ahead. If, that is, we still have sufficient time to undertake it.

NOTES

PREFATORY NOTE

1. See Gregory B. Lee, *Chinas Unlimited: Making the Imaginaries of China and Chineseness*, London: Routledge/Honolulu: Hawaii University Press, 2003; and Gregory B. Lee, *The Eighth Chinese Merchant and the Disappeared Chinese Seamen*, iBook, 2015, https://itunes.apple.com/fr/book/the-eighth-chinese-merchant/id1044441047?mt=11 (last accessed 12 September 2018).

INTRODUCTION

1. Wolfgang Behr implies that unification by the Qin is the moment at which China comes into existence, and describes what precedes it as 'the territories that we anachronistically call "China"'. See Wolfgang Behr, 'Role of Language in Early Chinese Constructions of Ethnic Identity', *Journal of Chinese Philosophy* 37:4 (December 2010), pp. 567–87.
2. *Relación del viaje que hezimos a la China desde la ciudad de Manila en las del Poniente, año de 1575, con mandado y acuerdo de Guido Lavazaris, Gouernador y Captan. general q. a la sazon era en las Islas Philiphinas.*
3. '*[L]a imagen de China se fue creando lentamente, mediante retazos de memoria, mediante experiencias personales, que darían lugar a visiones específicas de lo chino*'. Beatriz Moncó, 'Entre la imagen y la realidad: los viajes a China de Miguel de Loarca y Adriano de las Cortes', in *Revista Española del Pacífico*, núm. 8. Año VII. (1998), pp. 469–70. See also the work of Manel Ollé, *La invención de China: percepciones y estrategias filipinas respecto a China durante el siglo XVI*, Wiesbaden: Harrassowitz, 2000, on the importance of the Philippines as a site of stories and information from which the Spanish imaginary of China was constructed.
4. Geoff Wade, 'The Polity of Yelang and the Origin of the Name "China"', *Sino-Platonic Papers* 188 (May 2009).
5. Ibid., p. 6.

6. Arthur H. Smith, *Chinese Characteristics*, Shanghai: *North China Herald* office, 1890/London: Kegan Paul, 1892, p. 133.
7. Jean Rodes, *À travers la Chine actuelle*, Paris: Fasquelle, 1932, p. 172: '*Le pouvoir de contrôle du cerveau étant ainsi moins développé chez le Chinois, celui-ci, en certaines circonstances d'excitation, est livré à tous les réflexes inconscients, incontrôlés, de l'automatisme médullaire … [on voit] dans ce fait, une cause irrémédiable d'infériorité de race, qui eût enchanté le comte de Gobineau.*'
8. For more on European and American racist stereotyping of China and the Chinese, see Lee, *Chinas Unlimited*, Chapter 2 ('Addicted, Demented, and Taken to the Cleaners: The White Invention and Representation of the "Chinaman"').
9. Mark C. Elliott, 'The Limits of Tartary: Manchuria in Imperial and National Geographies', *The Journal of Asian Studies* 59:3 (2000), p. 603.
10. Joseph Needham, with the research assistance of Wang Ling, *Science and Civilisation in China, Volume 1: Introductory Orientations*, London: The Syndics of the Cambridge University Press, 1954. The title in Chinese expresses the 'Chineseness' of the subject matter even more plainly: *Zhongguo kexue jishu shi* 中國科學技術史 [China Science and Technology History].
11. Ibid., p. 77.
12. Ibid., p. 76.

1. WHAT AND WHEN IS CHINA?

1. Dru C. Gladney, *Dislocating China: Reflections on Muslims, Minorities, and Other Subaltern Subjects*, London: Hurst & Company, 2004, p. 7.
2. 吾國語能否變為字母之語; 漢文所以不易普及者, 其故不在漢文, 而在教之之術之不完. See the entry for 26 August 1915 in Hu Shi 胡適, *Hu Shi liuxue riji* 胡適留學日記, Taiwan shangwu yinshuguan 臺灣商務印書館 1947; 1959, vol. 3, p. 759.

2. *ZHONGGUO* AND THE HISTORIC VOCABULARY OF NATIONALISM

1. Wolfgang Behr, '"To Translate" is "To Exchange"—Linguistic Diversity and the Terms for Translation in Ancient China', in Michael Lackner and Natascha Vittinghoff (eds), *Mapping Meanings: The Field of New Learning in Late Qing China*, Leiden: Brill, 2004, pp. 200–35.
2. Ibid., p. 202.
3. Ibid., p. 204.

4. Known simply as the *Shiji* 史記 in Chinese, literally 'Historical Records'. See Burton Watson's translation: *Ssu Ma Chien Grand Historian of China*, New York, NY: Columbia University Press, 1958.
5. Dru C. Gladney, *Muslim Chinese: Ethnic Nationalism in the People's Republic*, Cambridge, MA: Council on East Asian Studies, Harvard University Press, 1990, p. 82.
6. See 'Doc. 56. The manifesto of the T'ung Meng-hui, 1905' in Ssu-yü Têng and John K. Fairbank, *China's Response to the West: A Documentary Survey 1839–1923*, Cambridge, MA: Harvard University Press, 1954/ New York, NY: Atheneum, 1963, pp. 227–9. For much of the second half of the twentieth century, Fairbank was the doyen of American historians of China.
7. Mark C. Elliot, 'The Limits of Tartary: Manchuria in Imperial and National Geographies', *The Journal of Asian Studies* 59:3 (2000), pp. 603–46, which discusses the 'relation between the spatial identity of the Qing and that of modern China' in the context of the construction of a singular Manchu identity. However, what Elliot considers a 'reconstitution of national territory', I should describe as a first-time constitution of national territory. His conclusion in full (p. 640) is as follows: 'the geographical instantiation of the modern Chinese state involved, not so much the preservation of what was, in the end, a highly problematic legacy from the Qing, but the reconstitution of national territory. That this required a new imagination of the Chinese nation is obscured by the choice that was made in the end, namely, to rebuild on the lines of the Qing empire. But it was a reconstitution, nonetheless.'
8. Ibid., p. 640.
9. Timothy Brook gives 175 million in *The Confusions of Pleasure: Commerce and Culture in Ming China*, Berkeley, CA: University of California Press, 1998, p. 162, whereas J.K. Fairbank and Merle Goldman give a more conservative 160 million in *China: A New History*, Cambridge, MA: Harvard University Press, 2006, p. 128.
10. The Chinese historical geographer Ge Jianxiong claims that the Qing dynasty population peaked at 430 million in 1850 and fell dramatically, perhaps by as much as 100 million, after the Taiping Rebellion (1850–64), and that it was not until 1912 that the 1850 figure was reached once more. See Ge Jianxiong, 'Zhongguo lidai renkou shuliang de yanbian ji zengjian de yuanyin 葛剑雄, '中国历代人口数量的衍变及增减的原因' [Reasons for the rise and fall in China's historical population statistics], in *Dang de wenxian* 党的文献/*Literature of the Chinese Communist Party*, No. 2, 2008, p. 94.

11. Prasenjit Duara, 'Historical consciousness and national identity', in Kam Louie (ed.), *The Cambridge Companion to Modern Chinese Culture*, Cambridge: Cambridge University Press, 2008, p. 63.
12. 有歷史的人種, 有非歷史的人種.
13. Liang Qichao 梁啟超, 'Lishi yu renzhong zhi guanxi' 歷史與人種之關係 [The relation between race and history], *Yinbingshi wenji* 飲冰水文集, Taibei: Xinxing shudian 新興書店, 1955, Vol. 3, p. 111.
14. 中國人, 日本人 朝鮮人 暹羅 人, 其他亞細亞東部人; 蒙古人, 韃靼人, 鮮卑人 (即今西伯利亞人), 其他亞細亞北部中部之人; 土耳其人, 匈加利人, 其他在歐洲之黃種人.
15. Duara sees globalization as putting this territorial model under stress: 'The effort to integrate the overseas Han Chinese into the nation has led to a spatial reimagination of the nation from the territorial China to the ethnic one'. Duara in Louie, p. 63.
16. Sun Yat-sen, 'I. Race and Population: Lecture One, Delivered on January 27, 1924', *San Min Chu I: The Three Principles of The People*, https://sunyatsenfoundation.org/wpcore/wp-content/uploads/San-Min-Chu-I_FINAL-3-Principles.pdf (last accessed 20 April 2018); 因為中國自秦漢而後, 都是一個民族造成一個國家; 外國有一個民族造成幾個國家的, 有在一個國家之內有幾個民族的。像英國是現在世界上頂強的國家, 他們國內的民族是用白人為本位, 結合棕人黑人等民族, 才成「大不列顛帝國」; 所以在英國說民族就是國族, 這一句話便不適當。再像香港, 是英國的領土, 其中的民族, 有幾十萬人是中國的漢人參加在內; 如果說香港的英國國族就是民族, 便不適當', https://zh.wikisource.org/wiki/三民主義/民族主義第一講 (last accessed 20 April 2018).
17. Sun Yat-sen, '造成這種種民族的原因, 概括的說是自然力, 分析起來便很複雜, 當中最大的力是「血統」: 中國人黃色的原因, 是由於根源黃色血統而成。祖先是什麼血統, 便永遠遺傳成一族的人民, 所以血統的力是很大的', https://zh.wikisource.org/wiki/三民主義/民族主義第一講 (last accessed 20 April 2018). Author's translation.
18. 文化没有断过流, 始终传下来的只有中国的.我们这些人也是原来的人。黑头发, 黄皮肤, 传承下来. 我们叫龙的传人, CCTV 8 November 2017. See 'Trump gets schooled on Chinese history by Xi Jinping', posted by That's Online, 8 November 2017, https://www.youtube.com/watch?v=aF119qafXq0 (last accessed 20 April 2018).

3. CHINA, ITS AUTHORITIES AND THE NATIONAL IMAGINARY

1. '中国是一个世界历史最悠久的国家之一。中国各族人民共同创造了光辉灿烂的文化...' in *Zhonghua renmin gongheguoxianfa* 中華人民共和國宪法/'The Constitution of the People's Republic of China', Beijing: Falü chubanshe 法律出版社, 2003, pp. 3, 47.

2. 孔夫子有些好处, 但也不是很好的。我们认为应该讲公道话。秦始皇比孔夫子伟大得多。孔夫子是讲空话的。秦始皇是第一个把中国统一起来的人物, 不但政治上统一了中国, 而且统一了中国的文字、中国各种制度如度量衡, 有些制度后来一直沿用下来。中国过去的封建君主还没有第二个人超过他的。可是被人骂了几千年, 骂他就是两条: 杀了460个知识分子; 烧了一些书. Cited in Chen Bian 陈晋 (ed.), *Mao Zedong dushu biji jiexi* 毛泽东读书笔记解析 [Mao Zedong's reading notes and analyses], Guangzhou: Guangdong Renmin chubanshe 广东人民出版社,1996, xiace 下册, p. 1155.
3. This historical narrative is one to which current pro-government theoreticians gladly adhere. See Yu Keping, 'The Transformation of Chinese Culture since the Launching of Reform: A Historical Perspective', Theory China website, 27 August 2012, (11–06–2013), http://en.theorychina.org/xsqy_2477/201306/t20130611_270481.shtml (last accessed 20 April 2018).
4. See Chow Tse-tung, *The May Fourth Movement: Intellectual Revolution in Modern China*, Cambridge, MA: Harvard University Press, 1960, passim.
5. John Dewey, 'New Culture in China', *Asia* 21:7 (July 1921), p. 585, cited in Chow Tse-tung, pp. 182–3.
6. See Cornelius Castoriadis, *Fait et à faire. Les Carrefours du labyrinthe, Vol. V*, Paris: Seuil, 1997, p. 12 for the '*magma de significations imaginaires sociales*'. For a good analytical summary of Castoriadis's work, see N. Poirier, *Castoriadis: L'Imaginaire radical*, Paris: PUF, 2004; or David Curtis (ed. and trans.), *The Castoriadis Reader*, Oxford: Blackwell, 1997.

4. WOMEN IN NATIONALISM'S SNARE

1. Charlotte Furth, *A Flourishing Yin: Gender in China's Medical History, 960–1665*, Berkeley, CA/London: University of California Press, 1999, p. 268.
2. Ibid., p. 271.
3. Susan Mann, 'The Education of Daughters in the Mid-Ch'ing Period', in Benjamin A. Elman and Alexander Woodside (eds), *Education and Society in Late Imperial China, 1600–1900*, Berkeley, CA/London: University of California Press, 1994, pp. 23–4.
4. Ibid., p. 24.
5. Ibid., pp. 37–8.
6. Ibid., p. 38.
7. Cited in Chow, *The May Fourth Movement*, p. 34.
8. Hsiung Ping-chen, 'Constructed Emotions: The Bond between Mothers and Sons in Late Imperial China', *Late Imperial China* 15:1 (June 1994),

pp. 97–9, cited in Benjamin A. Elman, *A Cultural History of Civil Examinations in Late Imperial China*, Berkeley, CA: University of California Press, 2000, p. 241.

9. Amy D. Dooling, *Women's Literary Feminism in Twentieth-Century China*, New York, NY: Palgrave Macmillan, 2005, p. 35.
10. Ibid., p. 48. Dooling adopts the more generous and indulgent position that nationalist discourse 'facilitated the construction of a new emancipatory discourse on women.'
11. Ibid., p. 64.
12. Megan M. Ferry, 'Woman and Her Affinity to Literature: Defining Women's Writers' Roles in China's Cultural Modernity', in Charles A. Laughlin (ed.), *Contested Modernities in Chinese Literature*, New York, NY: Palgrave Macmillan, 2005, p. 43.
13. Ibid., p. 43.
14. Tonglin Lu (ed.), *Gender and Sexuality in Twentieth-Century Chinese Literature and Society*, Albany, NY: State University of New York Press, 1993, p. 3. *The White-Haired Girl* 白毛女, written by pro-Communist playwright Tian Han 田漢 in the 1940s, was subsequently reproduced in several forms over the succeeding decades: revolutionary ballet, film and comic flick book.
15. Ibid., p. 3.
16. See C. T. Hsia, *A History of Modern Chinese Fiction*, New Haven, CT/London: Yale University Press, 1971 (second edition), Appendix 1, pp. 533–54; and Eileen Chang, *Love in a Fallen City*, Penguin Classics, London: Penguin Books Ltd., 2007.
17. Hsia, *History of Modern Chinese Fiction*, pp. 534–5.
18. Lu, *Gender and Sexuality*, pp. 1–2.

5. ILLITERACY AND THE CULTURAL IMAGINARY

1. David Johnson, 'Communication, Class and Consciousness in Late Imperial China', in David Johnson, Andrew J. Nathan and Evelyn S. Rawski (eds), *Popular Culture in Late Imperial China*, Berkeley, CA: University of California Press, 1985, p. 36, referring to research in Evelyn Rawski, *Education and Popular Literacy in Ch'ing China*, Ann Arbor, MI: University of Michigan Press, 1979, pp. 8–20.
2. Johnson, in Johnson, Nathan and Rawski (eds), *Popular Culture*, pp. 36–7.
3. Ibid., p. 38.
4. Ibid., p. 44.

5. Ibid., p. 38.
6. G. William Skinner (ed.), *The City in Late Imperial China*, Stanford, CA: Stanford University Press, 1977, pp. 225–6, cited in Johnson, Nathan and Rawski (eds), *Popular Culture*, p. 372. Skinner estimates the population in 1893 to be 394 million, and the urban population, those living in towns of over 2,000 inhabitants, as 6 per cent, or 23.5 million.
7. Leo Lee and Andrew J. Nathan, 'Beginnings of Mass Culture', in Johnson, Nathan and Rawski, *Popular Culture*, p. 361. According to the state's own figures (*Beijing Review*, 8 November 1982, 45:20), 38 per cent of China's population in 1964 was still illiterate, while in 1982 the figure stood at 23.5 per cent.
8. Mary Anderson, *Protestant Mission Schools for Girls in South China*, Mobile, AL: Heiter Starke Printing Company, 1943, pp. 27–8, cited in Mann, 'The Education of Daughters', p. 38.
9. Lee and Nathan, in Johnson, Nathan and Rawski (eds), *Popular Culture*, p. 361.
10. Ibid., p. 363.

6. CHINESE LANGUAGE?

1. Behr, 'Role of Language in Early Chinese Constructions of Ethnic Identity', p. 578.
2. '*Les caractères chinois sont souvent présentés au public étranger comme de petits dessins, et il ne manque pas de sinisants pour conforter ce phantasme. Il suffit de montrer à des personnes n'ayant jamais appris le chinois quelques caractères, pris au hasard, ou même choisis pour leur prétendue ressemblance avec le référent du mot qu'ils désignent, pour constater que le sens leur restera mystérieux. Les tenants de la thèse pictographique répondront que cette opacité résulte de l'évolution de l'écriture et qu'à l'origine, sur les plastrons de tortue ou les bronzes, on avait bien des images. Une personne ignorant le chinois à qui l'on présenterait ces formes, exactement reproduites d'après les originaux et sans lui dire la signification des mots en question, ne la devinera pas plus que dans le cas des caractères contemporains. Les textes archaïques chinois ne sont nullement des suites d'images: ils sont constitués de véritables phrases comportant des mots grammaticaux et construites selon un ordre défini.*' Viviane Alleton, *L'Écriture chinoise: Le défi de la modernité*, Paris: Éditions Albin Michel, 2008, p. 221.
3. See Bernhard Karlgren, *Grammata Serica: Script and Phonetics in Chinese and Sino-Japanese*, Stockholm: The Museum of Far Eastern Antiquities, 1940.
4. William H. Baxter and Laurent Sagart, *Old Chinese: A New Reconstruction*, Oxford/New York: Oxford University Press, 2014.

5. *Tangshi sanbai shou* 唐詩三百首 [Three Hundred Tang Poems], Taibei: Dazhong shuju 大眾書局, 1976, p. 154.
6. There are numerous translations of this poem. One study in particular has attempted to show the variety of translations possible: Octavio Paz and Eliot Weinberger, *19 Ways of Looking at Wang Wei*, New York, NY: New Directions, 1987, 2016. See also Sidney Wade, '13 Ways of Looking at Wang Wei', *Subtropics* 20:21 (Spring/Summer 2016), pp. 174–8.
7. Wang Wei and G. W. Robinson (trans.), *Poems of Wang Wei*, Harmondsworth: Penguin, 1974.
8. Burton Watson, *Chinese Lyricism: Shih Poetry from the Second to the Twelfth Century, with translations*, New York, NY/London: Columbia University Press, 1971, p. 10.
9. Ibid., pp. 10–11.
10. Ibid., p. 12.
11. Duo Duo, *The Boy Who Catches Wasps*, trans. Gregory B. Lee, Brookline, MA: Zephyr Press, 2002, p. 31.
12. Ibid., p. 30.

7. THE MAKING OF A NATIONAL LANGUAGE

1. '*Gesheng liu Hu xuesheng zonghui diyize jianzhang*' 各省留滬學生總會第一則簡章 [First Draft programme of the Alliance of Students in Shanghai from All Provinces], 1906 in 江寧 學務 *Jiangning xuewu* [Educational Affairs of Jiangning prefecture], Nanjing, 1906, cited in Chow, p. 34.
2. Chow, p. 279.
3. See Ping Chen, 'Languages in a modernizing China', in Kam Louie (ed.), *The Cambridge Companion to Modern Chinese Culture*, Cambridge: Cambridge University Press, 2008, pp. 206–7.
4. See Jian Zhao, 'Japanese Loanwords in Modern Chinese', *Journal of Chinese Linguistics* 34:2 (June 2006), pp. 306–27.
5. Shouyi Fan, 'Highlights of Translation Studies in China Since the Mid-Nineteenth Century', *Meta* 44:1 (March 1999), p. 2, id.erudit.org/iderudit/002716ar (last accessed 8 June 2018).
6. See Paul Kratochvíl, *The Chinese Language Today*, London: Hutchinson University Library, 1968, p. 20: 'The classical written style … represented the norm of writing, and *guanhua* "officials' language", also known as Mandarin, was used, although in a much narrower sense than European standard languages, as the norm of oral communication.'
7. Chow, p. 44, note d states: 'The French title *La Jeunesse* was attached from

the issue of Jan. 1919 (Vol. VI, No. 1)'. This is inaccurate, as a glance at the 1915 cover (see Fig. 3) demonstrates.

8. In January 1920, the Ministry of Education decided that the vernacular would be used in the first two years of primary education, and the adoption of the vernacular quickly spread to higher echelons of the school system. In 1920–1, the northern vernacular was officially recognized as the 'national language' (*Guoyu* 國語). Chow, p. 279.
9. See the essay 'Jianshe de wenxue geming lu' 建設的文學革命論 [Constructive revolution in Chinese literature], Hu Shi 胡適, *Hu Shi wencun* 胡適文存, Taibei: Yuangong tushu gongsi 遠東圖書公司, 1953, Vol. 1, pp. 55, 57: '有了這種『真文學』和『活文學』, 那些『假文學』和『死文學』自然會消滅了....我們所提倡的文學革命, 只是要替中國創造—種國語的文學。有了國語的文學, 方才可有文學的國語。有了文學的國語我們的國語才可算得真正國語。國語沒有文學, 便沒有生命, 便沒有價值, 便不能成立, 便不能發達'.
10. Pierre Bourdieu, *Sur l'État: Cours au Collège de France (1989–1992)*, Paris: Seuil, 2012, pp. 193–4: '*Cette unification du marché linguistique, cette unification du marché de l'écriture qui est coextensive à l'État, c'est l'État qui la fait en se faisant. C'est une des manières pour l'État de se faire que de faire de l'orthographe, normalisée, que de faire les poids et mesures normalisés, que de faire le droit normalisé … le système scolaire, un processus par lequel on fait aussi des individus normalisés qui sont homogénéisés du point de vue de l'écriture, de l'orthographe, de la manière de parler*'.
11. See Chang-tai Hung, *Going to the People: Chinese Intellectuals and Folk Literature, 1918–1937*, Harvard, MA: The Council on East Asian Studies, Harvard University, 1985, p. 63.
12. Leo K. Shin, *The Making of the Chinese State: Ethnicity and Expansion on the Ming Borderlands*, New York, NY: Cambridge University Press, 2006, p. xiii.
13. William C. Kirby, 'China's Prosperous Age: A Century in the Making', *China Heritage Quarterly* 26 (June 2011), http://www.chinaheritagequarterly.org/features.php?searchterm=026_kirby.inc&issue=026 (last accessed 17 February 2018); and Kirby, 'When Did China Become China? Thoughts on the Twentieth Century', in Joshua A. Fogel (ed.), *The Teleology of the Modern Nation-State*, Philadelphia, PA: University of Pennsylvania Press, 2005, pp. 105–14.
14. For a brief yet erudite discussion of alternative names for Hoklo—Fúlǎo 福佬/Héluò 河洛 (Hoklo), Táiyǔ 台語 (Taiwanese), *Taiwanhua* 台灣話 (Taiwanese)—see Victor Mair, 'Hoklo', *Language Log*, 18 September 2016 http://languagelog.ldc.upenn.edu/nll/?p=28211 (last accessed 18 April 2018).

15. *Gu* 古 was in common use before the twentieth century in the term *guwen* 古文. Used by the Tang 唐 dynasty prose writer Han Yu 韓愈 (786–824), it denoted a didactic genre of writing. *Guwen* 古文, which may be translated as 'old text' or 'ancient prose', referred to prose found in the philosophical classics, the writings of the Tang and Song masters. For Song Neo-Confucians writing was a vehicle of the way (*wen yi zai dao* 文以載道), and *guwen* was more than a style—it was 'ideologically grounded in the Confucian Classics'. See Kai-wing Chow, 'Discourse, Examination, and Local Elite', in Benjamin A. Elman and Alexander Woodside (eds), *Education and Society in Late Imperial China*, Berkeley, CA/London: University of California Press, 1994, pp. 186–7.
16. Arthur Waley (ed.), *Chinese Poems*, London: George Allen and Unwin, 1946.
17. Paul Demiéville, *Anthologie de la poésie chinoise classique* [Anthology of Classical Chinese Poetry], Paris: Gallimard, 1962.
18. Ding Xuxin and Burton Raffel, *Gems of Chinese Poetry: Zhongguo shige jinghua* 中國詩歌精华, Shenyang: Liaoning University Press 辽宁大学出版社, 1986.
19. Craig Clunas, *Chinese Painting and Its Audiences*, Princeton, NJ: Princeton University Press, 2017.
20. '[Japanese early twentieth-century] valuation [of the newly imported Yuan and Ming dynasty works] was intrinsically linked to a view of China as marked by past cultural achievements, with the centre of Eastern culture now having moved decisively to Japan'. Ibid., p. 163.
21. Ibid., p. 164.
22. '[I]n the twentieth century *guo* [國] would become indelibly associated with the concept of nation. It would later come to be associated with *hua* [畫] "painting", in the neologism *guohua* [國畫], "national painting" (derived from the Japanese equivalent *kokuga*), in the sense of a form of painting that is distinctive to and unique to the Chinese nation, which embodies some sort of essence of Chinese culture.' Ibid., p. 172.
23. Ibid., p. 163.
24. See the very useful summaries of Bridie Andrews, *The Making of Modern Chinese Medicine, 1850–1960*, Vancouver: UBC Press, 2014 and of Sean Hsiang-Lin Lei, *Neither Donkey Nor Horse: Medicine in the Struggle Over China's Modernity*, Chicago, IL: University of Chicago Press, 2014, in Lijing Jiang's review essay, 'The old, the new and the state in the making of modern East Asian medicine', *Studies in the History and Philosophy of Biological and Biomedical Sciences* 64 (2017), pp. 88–91.

25. The dominance of Western medicine in today's world is simply illustrated by it alone being referred to just as 'medicine'—scientific, universal, unqualified, while everyone else's must be qualified as an ethnic or alternative medicine.
26. '*[L]a création a toujours lieu* dans *le déjà-là et* par *les moyens, aussi, que celui-ci offre. Cela ne l'empêche pas d'être création en tant que forme*.' Cornelius Castoriadis, *Fait et à faire. Les Carrefours du labyrinthe*, *Vol. V*, Paris: Seuil, 1997, p. 223.
27. 《沁園春》赴密州, 早行, 馬上寄子由: 當時共客長安 似二陸初來俱少年 有筆頭千字 胸中萬卷 致君堯舜 此事何難 用舍由時 行藏在我 袖手何妨閑處看 身長健 但優游卒歲 且鬥樽前. My translation.
28. *Mao Tse-tung Poems*, Peking: Foreign Language Press, 1976. 携来百侣曾游, 忆往昔峥嵘岁月稠。恰同学少年, 风华正茂; 书生意气, 挥斥方遒。指点江山, 激扬文字, 粪土当年万户侯。曾记否, 到中流击水, 浪遏飞舟!
29. Cyril Birch, 'Foreword', in Andrew H. Plaks (ed.), *Chinese Narrative: Critical and Theoretical Essays*, Princeton, NJ: Princeton University Press, 1977, p. xi.
30. Ibid., p. xi.
31. Ibid., pp. xi–xii.
32. See the chapters 'Story-Tellers' Prompt-Books of the Sung Dynasty' ['Song zhi hua ben' '宋之話本] and 'Imitations of Prompt-Books in the Sung and Yuan Dynasties' [Song Yuan zhi si hua ben' 宋元之似話], in Lu Hsun [Lu Xun], *A Brief History of Chinese Fiction*, trans. Yang Hsien-yi and Gladys Yang, Peking: Foreign Languages Press, 1976, pp. 131–42, 143–53. For the text in Chinese, see Lu Xun 魯迅, *Zhongguo xiaoshuo shilüe* 中國小說史略, in *Lu Xun quanji* 魯迅全集 [Lu Xun's Complete Works], vol. 8, Hong Kong: Xianggang wenxue yanjiushe 香港文學研究社, 1973, pp. 85–93, 94–100.
33. Vibeke Boerdahl, *The Eternal Storyteller: Oral Literature in Modern China*, NIAS Studies in Asia Topics, 24, London: Routledge, 1998, p. 37.
34. Ibid.
35. '中国之小说自来無史; 有之, 則先見于外国人所作之中国文学史中', *Lu Xun quanji* 魯迅全集, vol. 8, p. 4.
36. Lu Hsun, Preface to *A Brief History of Chinese Fiction*.
37. Herbert G. Giles, *A History of Chinese Literature*, New York/London: D. Appleton and Company, 1901, p. xvii.
38. Ibid.
39. Birch in Plaks, p. xi.
40. Ibid., p. x.
41. See Mau-sang Ng, *The Russian Hero in Modern Chinese Fiction*, Hong Kong/

New York, NY: Chinese University Press/State University of New York Press, 1988, passim.

42. Charles J. Alber, 'Introduction', in V.I. Semanov, *Lu Hsün and his predecessors* (ed. and trans. Charles J. Alber), White Plains, NY: M. E. Sharpe, 1980, pp. xxii–iii. For the translated stories of Lu Xun, see Gladys Yang (ed. and trans.), *Silent China: Selected Writings of Lu Xun*, London/Oxford/New York, NY: Oxford University Press, 1973.
43. Guo Moruo, *Luoye*, Shanghai: Chuangzaoshe 創造社, 1926; Lao She, *Lao Zhang de zhexue* [Lao Zhang's Philosophy], in *Xiaoshuo yuebao* 小說月報 17:7–12 (July 1926-December 1926) and Shanghai: Shanghai yinshuguan 上海印書館, January 1928; Ba Jin, *Miewang* in *Xiaoshuo yuebao* 小說月報 20:1–4 (January 1929-April 1929) and Shanghai: Kaiming shudian 開明書店, 1929; Ding Ling, *Shui* [Flood *or* Water], in *Beidou* 北斗 1:1–1:3 (20 September 1931–20 November 1931) and Shanghai: Xin Zhongguo shuju 新中國書局, 1933.
44. Ping Chen, in Louie, pp. 202–3.
45. Vibeke Børdahl, Fei Li, and Huang Ying, *Four Masters of Chinese Storytelling: Full-length Repertoires of Yangzhou Storytelling on Video/Yangzhou pinghua sijia yiren: Quanshu biaoyan luxiang mulu* 揚州評話四家藝人: 全書表演錄像目錄 [Bilingual ed.], Copenhagen, NIAS Press, 2004, p. 1.
46. '*Cet événement a eu des conséquences directes sur le développement du tourisme dans la région et sur la valorisation culturelle du théâtre de Guan Suo, aboutissant en 2011 à sa reconnaissance comme « patrimoine culturel immatériel national » (Zhongguo feiwuzhi wenhua yichan* 中国非物质文化遗产*).*' Sylvie Beaud, 'La fabrique d'un patrimoine chinois: d'une production culturelle nationale à une tradition théâtrale locale' [The Making of a Chinese Heritage: From a National Cultural Production to a Local Theatrical Tradition], *Ebisu: Etudes japonaises* 52 (2015), 'Patrimonialisation et identités en Asie orientale', p. 52.
47. '*Au terme de ce processus de réappropriation et de médiatisation, une ressource culturelle essentiellement locale est ainsi devenue patrimoine national*'. Beaud, pp. 294–5.
48. '[*L*]*e théâtre de masques sert également à construire une image de la Chine vue de l'étranger, notamment à travers le regard du personnage japonais. Le film donne à voir une ruralité naïve et ethnicisée tout en étant détentrice de savoirs ancestraux: le cinéaste exploite l'esthétique de l'architecture ancienne, de la nature et du théâtre de masques. Cette image stéréotypée du Yunnan et de ses habitants reflète cependant aussi le regard des Chinois eux-mêmes, puisque la province se promeut par les mêmes emblèmes (ethnicité, ancestralité, faune et flore luxuriantes, paysages grandioses).*' Beaud, p. 298.
49. Or, as Beaud has it (p. 298), a certain kind of 'internal Orientalism' '*une certaine forme d'orientalisme interne*'.

50. '*La fabrique du patrimoine résulte donc ici d'un mouvement vertical: émanant du national par le biais d'une production artistique qui fait office d'accélérateur, suscitant en retour des initiatives au niveau local, pour « remonter » ensuite vers le national et les autorités compétentes pour attribuer les labels. Ce bien culturel devient de fait un patrimoine d'État, que chaque Chinois peut dès lors s'approprier.*' Beaud, p. 318.
51. Gregory B. Lee, *China's Lost Decade: Cultural Politics and Poetics 1978–1990—In place of history*, Brookline, MA/Lyon: Zephyr Press/Tigre de papier, 2012, p. 189; and *State Statistical Bureau, Statistical Yearbook of China*, 1992, cited in Paul Bowles and Xiao-yuan Dong, 'Current Successes and Future Challenges in China's Economic Reforms', *New Left Review* 208 (1994), p. 50.
52. For a more complete critique of the song and video featuring Gao Feng 高枫, see Gregory B. Lee, *Chinas Unlimited: Making the Imaginaries of China and Chineseness*, London/Honolulu: Routledge/Hawaii University Press, 2003, Chapter 3: 'Re-Taking Tiger Mountain by Television: Televisual Socialization of the Chinese Consumer'.
53. See E.J. Hobsbawm, *Nations and Nationalism Since 1780: Programme, Myth, Reality* (London/New York: Cambridge University Press, 1991), passim; and my discussion of his argument in Gregory B. Lee, *Troubadours, Trumpeters, Troubled Makers: Lyricism, Nationalism, and Hybridity in China and Its Others*, London/Durham, NC: C. Hurst & Co/Duke University Press, 1996, p. 172. While Hobsbawm accepts that French as a national language was imposed on the inhabitants of the space called 'France' by the regnant revolutionary authority, he still sees the 'nation' as a vehicle to achieve a more progressive society. Nevertheless, he also insists that 'no serious historian of nations and nationalism can be a committed political nationalist', since nationalism 'requires too much belief in what is patently not so' (p. 12).
54. Amnesty International UK, 'China: Tibetan activist faces 15 years after appearing in New York Times film', press release, 4 January 2018, https://www.amnesty.org.uk/press-releases/china-tibetan-activist-faces-15-years-after-appearing-new-york-times-film (last accessed 21 February 2018).

8. CHINA-BEFORE-CHINA REVISITED

1. Luo Yunzhou, 'Chinese civilization proven extra ancient', *Global Times*, 28 January 2018, http://www.globaltimes.cn/content/1086957.shtml (last accessed 28 February 2018).

2. Hui Li, Ying Huang, Laura F. Mustavich et al., 'Y chromosomes of prehistoric people along the Yangtze River', *Human Genetics*, 122:3–4 (November 2007), p. 383.
3. Ibid.

9. READING CHINESE

1. I thank my colleague and friend Iain Chambers for sharing this insight with me. See his *Postcolonial Interruptions, Unauthorised Modernities*, London: Rowman & Littlefield International, 2017.
2. At the author's own university, Jean Moulin-Lyon, the number of students enrolling in Korean language courses has increased dramatically in recent years, even overtaking the demand for Japanese, while Chinese comes in a poor third: 'Université Jean-Moulin-Lyon-III got 667 … applications [for Korean] or a competition ratio of 10 to 1.' In Parisian institutions, the numbers are even higher: 'Last September [2017], 1,056 students applied to Paris-VII University's Korean Studies Department, which only has a quota of about 100, while 1,014 applied at INALCO, which has a quota of 150. The competition is even fiercer for the new academic year that starts this September [2018]. College applications data show that 1,412 and 1,360 students applied to the two [programmes in total].' *The Chosulnibo*, 'More and more French university students are applying to Korean studies departments', 9 April 2018, http://english.chosun.com/site/data/html_dir/2018/04/09/2018040901290.html (last accessed 27 July 2018).

10. VERSAILLES

1. See Gregory B. Lee, *The Eighth Chinese Merchant and the Disappeared Chinese Seamen*, iBook, 2015, https://itunes.apple.com/gb/book/the-eighth-chinese-merchant/id1044441047?mt=11 (last accessed 12 September 2018).
2. For more on the impact of the Versailles peace treaty, see Gregory B. Lee, *Troubadours, Trumpeters, Troubled Makers: Lyricism, Nationalism, and Hybridity in China and Its Others*, London/Durham, NC: C. Hurst & Co/Duke University Press, 1996, pp. 68–70.
3. Frank Füredi, *The New Ideology of Imperialism*, London/Boulder, CO: Pluto Press, 1994, p. 5.
4. '*[I]l fallait au nom de la Science détruire les idées fausses, les religions, les traditions culturelles, les mythes, tout cela, produits de l'imagination dans les âges obscurs, devait absolument être remplacé par la Lumière de la Science.*' Jacques Ellul, *Le Bluff technologique*, Paris: Fayard/Pluriel, 2010, p. 323.

11. WESTERN 'VALUES'?

1. Deng Xiaoping, 'Take a Clear-Cut Stand against Bourgeois Liberalization', in Deng Xiaoping, *Fundamental Issues in Present-Day China*, Beijing: Foreign Languages Press, 1989. For a discussion of the these two campaigns see Gregory B. Lee, *China's Lost Decade: Cultural Politics and Poetics 1978–1990—In place of history*, Brookline, MA/Lyon: Zephyr Press; Lyon: Tigre de papier, 2012, pp. 177–81.
2. 特别是一些西方国家利用长期积累的经济科技优势和话语强势, 对外推销以所谓"普世价值"为内核的思想文化, 企图诱导人们"以西为美", "唯西是从", 淡化乃至放弃对本民族精神文化的认同。党的十九大报告强调, 文化是一个国家、一个民族的灵魂.... Huang Kunming 黄坤明, 'Peiyu he jianxing shehuizhuyi kexin jiazhiguan' 培育和践行社会主义核心价值观 [Cultivate and implement socialist core values], *Zhongguo gongchandang xinwen* 中国共产党新闻 [Chinese Communist Party News], 17 November 2017, http://cpc.people.com.cn/n1/2017/1117/c64094-29651333.html (last accessed 21 February 2018). Author's translation.
3. Jacques Ellul, *Changer de révolution* [For a different revolution], Paris: La Table Ronde, 2015.
4. A Suzhou scholar, Feng Guifen 馮桂芬 (1809–74), was reputedly the first person to employ the term 'self-strengthening'. See Teng and Fairbank, *China's Response to the West*, p. 50. It was Zhang Zhidong 張之洞 (1837–1909), known as one of the four celebrated officals of the late Qing, who popularized the *Zhongxue wei ti, Xixue wei yong* slogan in 1898; the other three, all generals, were Zeng Guofan 曾國藩 (1811–72), Li Hongzhang 李鴻章 (1823–1901) and Zuo Zongtang 左宗棠 (1812–85).
5. See the recent critique of France's policy of exploiting the French language through what is known as La Francophonie. Angelique Chrisafis, 'Macron's French language crusade bolsters imperialism—Congo novelist: Club of French-speaking countries needs total overhaul, says novelist Alain Mabanckou', *The Guardian*, 19 February 2018, https://www.theguardian.com/world/2018/feb/19/emmanuel-macron-challenged-over-attitude-to-frances-former-colonies?CMP=share_btn_tw (last accessed 21 February 2018). It is the business of the Confucius Institute network (the *Hanban* 汉办) to disseminate abroad the state's version of Chinese Confucian culture; it is fair to say that to date it has not been a huge success.

12. MODERN, MODERNITY, MODERNIZATION: EQUIVALENCE, TOTALIZATION AND BELONGING

1. See in particular the writings of the Qinghua-based academic Wang Hui 汪辉.
2. *The Millenial Quartet*: 1, *Alternative Modernities* (ed. Dilip Parameshwar Gaonkar), *Public Culture*, 11:1 (1999); 2, *Globalization*, ed. Arjun Appadurai, *Public Culture*, vol. 12, no. 1, 2000; 3, *Millennial Capitalism and Neo-Liberal Culture*, ed. Jean and John Comaroff, *Public Culture*, vol. 12, no. 2, 2000; 4. *Cosmopolitanism*, ed. Carol A. Breckenridge, Sheldon Pollock, Homi K. Bhabha and Dipesh Chakrabarty, *Public Culture*, vol. 12, no. 3, 2000.
3. Harry Harootunian, 'Quartering the Millennium' in *Radical Philosophy: A Journal of Socialist and Feminist Philosophy*, no. 166 (November/December 1999), pp. 21–29.
4. Arjun Appadurai, *Modernity at Large: Cultural Dimensions of Globalization*, Minneapolis, University of Minnesota Press, 2000.
5. Harry Harootunian, *Radical Philosophy*, no. 166, p. 22.
6. Ibid., no. 166, p. 22.
7. Ibid., no. 166, p. 24.
8. Ibid., no. 166, p. 27.
9. Karl Marx and Frederick Engels, with an Introduction by A. J. P. Taylor *The Communist Manifesto*, Harmondsworth, Middlesex: Penguin Books, 1967, p. 83–84.
10. Ibid., p. 84.
11. Holland Hunter, 'Tracking Economic Change with Ambiguous Tools: Soviet Planning, 1928–1991', *The Journal of Economic History* Vol. 58, No. 4 (Dec., 1998), p. 1027.
12. Jinglian Wu, *China's Long March Toward a Market Economy*, San Francisco, CA: Long River Press, 2005, Honolulu, Hawaii, 2009, p. 18n7.
13. Ibid., p. 18.
14. *The Communist Manifesto*, p. 84.
15. Roland Robertson, 'Comments on the "Global Triad" and "Glocalization"', in Nobutaka Inoue (ed.), *Globalization and Indigenous Culture: 40th anniversary memorial symposium*, Tokyo: Institute for Japanese Culture and Classics, Kokugakuin University, 1997, available at http://www2.kokugakuin.ac.jp/ijcc/wp/global/15robertson.html (last accessed 20 April 2018). 'The articles written in that period of the late '80s by Japanese economists sometimes employed the word "glocalization,"

which is usually rendered in Japanese … as *dochakuka*. This is a word, incidently, which has played an increasingly important part in my own writings, recently, about globalization. Because "glocalization" means the simultaneity,—the co-presence—of both universalizing and particularizing tendencies.'

16. Harry Harootunian, 'Quartering the Millennium', *Radical Philosophy* 116 (2002), p. 27.
17. Ibid., p. 28. Emphasis in original.
18. Ibid., pp. 28–9.
19. Walter D. Mignolo, *Local Histories/Global Designs: Coloniality, Subaltern Knowledges, and Border Thinking*, Princeton, NJ: Princeton University Press, 2000, passim.
20. 近代歐洲之所以優越他族者, 科學之興. Chen Duxiu 陳獨秀, 'Jinggao qingnian' 敬告青年 [literally 'Warning to Youth', often translated as 'Call to Youth'], *Xin qingnian* 新青年 1:1 (September 1915).
21. 凡此無常識之思惟, 無理由之信仰, 欲根治之, 厥為科學.
22. '在昔蒙昧之世，當今淺化之民，有想象而無科學。宗教美文，皆想象時代之產物' Chen Duxiu 陳獨秀, 'Jinggao qingnian' 敬告青年.

13. CHINA AND THE GLOBAL TECHNOLOGICO-ECONOMIC SYSTEM

1. See Siegfried Kracauer, *The Mass Ornament: Weimar Essays*, ed. & trans. Thomas Y. Levin, Harvard, MA: Harvard University Press, 1995.
2. See Gregory B. Lee, *Troubadours, Trumpeters, Troubled Makers: Lyricism, Nationalism, and Hybridity in China and Its Others*, London/Durham, NC: C. Hurst & Co./Duke University Press, 1996.
3. See Gregory B. Lee, 'Le cadeau empoisonné de Versailles ou La Chine à la manivelle de l'orgue de barbarie', *Mouvements* 72 (2012), pp. 79–88.
4. Jacques Ellul, *Le Système technicien*, Paris: Le Cherche Midi, 2012, p. 93.
5. Ibid., p. 100.
6. Ellul, *Changer de révolution*, p. 227: '*La technique en tant que modèle et en tant qu'idéologie a produit ses premiers fruits dans la qualité remarquable des jeunes Chinois scientifiques et techniciens que nous recevons maintenant en Occident où ils viennent se perfectionner et se situer … L'orientation actuelle est cohérente à la réalité. Mais elle exprime aussi cette réalité, à savoir que la technique a finalement vaincu le modèle révolutionnaire du communisme chinois. Cette interprétation nous permet d'éviter une erreur très fréquente qui se développe depuis trois ans. Tous les journaux français parlent de la « libéralisation du régime ». Or nous pensons qu'il s'agit d'une incompréhension*

de fond. Les observateurs partant avec cette idée sont alors tout surpris lorsque qu'on assiste à l'arrestation des gens qui affichent des dazibaos, *à des répressions de manifestations étudiantes ou ouvrières … Chaque fois on écrit: « coup de frein à la libéralisation. » Mais c'est un contresens. Il n'y a jamais eu de la libéralisation et la nouvelle tendance n'a rien à voir avec la liberté. Il y a passage d'un système où l'idéologie révolutionnaire primait le souci d'efficacité technique, à un système où la volonté de croissance technique efface l'idéologie révolutionnaire. La technique à tout prix et « l'efficacité d'abord » n'ont rien à voir avec la libéralisation'.*

7. Ellul, *Le Système technicien*, p. 305 & p. 305, n. 25.
8. Cornelius Castoriadis, *Histoire et création: Textes philosophiques inédits (1945–1967)*, Paris: Seuil, 2009, pp. 263–7.
9. Jacques Ellul, *Le Bluff technologique*, Paris: Fayard/Pluriel, 2012, pp. 332–7.
10. '*L'idéologie actuelle de la science est une idéologie du Salut.*' Ibid., p. 339.
11. '*L'univers dans lequel nous vivons devient de plus en plus rêvé, car la société du spectacle se change peu à peu en société du rêve.*' Ibid., p. 343.

14. XI'S 'CHINA DREAM', TECHNOLOGICAL NIGHTMARE AND 'HOODLUM DIPLOMACY'

1. For a survey of how sinology and Asian area studies, in general, have objectified China and Asia as a whole, see Gregory Lee, 'Taking Asia for an Object—The Big Mis-Take', *EastAsiaNet.eu Workshop: Mistaking Asia*, May 2008, Leeds, United Kingdom, available at https://halshs.archives-ouvertes.fr/halshs-00322535 (last accessed 31 July 2018).
2. Ai Weiwei, 'The refugee crisis isn't about refugees. It's about us', *The Guardian*, 2 February 2018, https://www.theguardian.com/commentisfree/2018/feb/02/refugee-crisis-human-flow-ai-weiwei-china (last accessed 25 February 2018).
3. Gregory Lee, Claire Dodane and Florent Villard, 'Arrest of Professor Ilham Tohti—French academics react', *Mediapart: Les blogs*, 27 February 2014, https://blogs.mediapart.fr/gblee/blog/270214/arrest-professor-ilham-tohti-french-academics-react (last accessed 10 July 2018). Tohti was found guilty of advocating separatism and jailed for life on 23 September 2014. In 2017 he was awarded the Weimar Human Rights Award; see Hans Spross, 'German award for Ilham Tohti sheds light on China's Uighur abuse', *Deutsche Welle*, http://www.dw.com/en/german-award-for-ilham-tohti-sheds-light-on-chinas-uighur-abuse/a-41712008 (last accessed 25 February 2018).

4. See Amnesty International, 'China: Authorities' revelations on detained Hong Kong booksellers "smoke and mirrors"', 5 February 2016, https://www.amnesty.nl/actueel/china-authorities-revelations-on-detained-hong-kong-booksellers-smoke-and-mirrors (last accessed 10 February 2018).
5. *The Basic Law of the Hong Kong Special Administrative Region of the People's Republic of China* (1990; effective 1 July 1997), Article 2, says this: 'The National People's Congress authorizes the Hong Kong Special Administrative Region to exercise a high degree of authority and enjoy executive, legislative and independent judicial power'.
6. Cottee, 'China's nuclear ambitions run into friction'.
7. See Karl H. Dannenfeldt, 'Sleep: Theory and Practice in the Late Renaissance', *Journal of the History of Medicine*, 41:4 (October 1986), p. 432: 'By the Renaissance, physicians had been aware for millennia of the nocturnal phenomenon known as the nightmare.' The ancient Greek physicians sought a natural physical cause for the visits of Ephialtes, the 'leaper', also called the Pnigalion, or the 'throttler'. In the Middle Ages, theologians converted the Incubus into a fiend of hell who terrified human beings and had intercourse with the sleeper.
8. Ellul, *Changer de révolution*, p. 227: '*Il n'y a jamais eu de la libéralisation et la nouvelle tendance n'a rien à voir avec la liberté.*'
9. Debord, 'La Société du spectacle', in *Œuvres*, p. 771: '*C'est la plus vieille spécialisation sociale, la spécialisation du pouvoir, qui est à la racine du spectacle. Le spectacle est ainsi une activité spécialisée qui parle pour l'ensemble des autres. C'est la représentation diplomatique de la société hiérarchique devant elle-même, où toute autre parole est bannie. Le plus moderne y est aussi le plus archaïque.*'
10. Witness also the criticism of the Chinese delegates' behaviour at the 2018 Pacific Island forum. The PRC delegation head was accused of 'disrespect' in storming out after trying to speak before Pacific leaders, amidst talk of big countries 'buying their way through the region'. See 'China must apologise for "arrogance" at Pacific summit, says Nauru president', SCMP 06 September 2018, 10.53pm. https://www.scmp.com/news/china/diplomacy/article/2163002/china-must-apologise-arrogance-pacific-summit-says-nauru (last consulted 9 September 2018).

15. TOWARDS A CONCLUSION

1. Kylie Korsnack, 'Transcending Boundaries: An Interview with Vandana Singh', *Los Angeles Review of Books*, 25 November 2017, https://lareviewof-

books.org/article/transcending-boundaries-an-interview-with-vandana-singh/ (last accessed 25 November 2017).

2. According to FAO 2017 statistics, citing a report by the Chinese Ministry of Environmental Protection and the Ministry of Land and Resources, 19.4 per cent of China's arable land is contaminated.
3. '[*C*]*e n'est pas l'illimité qui peut en rien fonder et constituer une culture, ni une personne … C'est en établissant des limites volontaires que l'homme s'institue homme*.' Ellul, *Le Système technicien*, p. 305, n. 25.
4. World Nuclear Association, 'Nuclear Power in China', updated July 2018, http://www.world-nuclear.org/information-library/country-profiles/countries-a-f/china-nuclear-power.aspx (last accessed 12 July 2018): 'Mainland China has over 40 nuclear power reactors in operation, about 20 under construction, and more about to start construction.'
5. Ellul, *Le Système technicien*, p. 304.
6. See Jenny Chan, 'Dying for an iPhone: The Labour Struggle of China's New Working Class', *Triple C Communication, Capitalism and Critique: Journal for a Global Sustainable Information Society* 12:2 (2014); and Yang, Jenny Chan, and Xu Lizhi, *La Machine est ton seigneur et ton maître*, Marseille: Agone, 2015.
7. Or, in French, '*éthique de la non-puissance*,' where the word *puissance* also implies capacity to do and not simply the political power to do. Ellul, *Changer de révolution*, p. 36.
8. '[*L*]*'esprit de Non-Puissance, qui dépasse la non-violence … est le choix … de ne pas dominer, de ne pas exploiter, de ne pas user même des moyens de puissance que l'on pourrait avoir*'. Ibid., p. 419.

16. CODA

1. '*[L]e fait décisif de la modernité: la technique fait triompher la raison instrumentale. La technique est beaucoup plus qu'un ensemble de procédés industriels, c'est un « procédé général », c'est à dire un imaginaire de pratiques tournées vers la production illimitée, l'efficacité et la multiplication de dispositifs abstraits et opprimants. Plongé dans un milieu qui n'est que moyens, intégralement médiatisé, et donc sans prise sur son environnement*, l'homo technologicus, *se retrouve dans un univers de fatalités où toutes les grandeurs (économie, médias, industrie, travail) le dépassent*.' Quentin Hardy, 'Introduction', in Bernard Charbonneau et Jacques Ellul, *Nous sommes des révolutionnaires malgré nous*, Paris: Seuil, 2014, p. 36.
2. '*[La technique] engendre le développement de la puissance. Loin de permettre l'émancipation, la puissance engendre des déséquilibres et devient incontrôlable, car elle*

appelle nécessairement la concentration et le gigantisme'. Charbonneau and Ellul, *Nous sommes des révolutionnaires malgré nous*, p. 36.

3. Ellul, *Le Système technicien*, p. 305, n. 25: '*Les seuils représentent les bornes entre lesquelles l'action de l'homme (et la technique) doit se situer pour que la survie reste possible. Il s'agit de nécessités. Et lorsque nous parlons de nuisances, de pollution, d'épuisement des ressources, nous désignons des seuils .... Il s'agit alors simplement des conditions de survie. Mais ceci n'est rien pour la création d'une civilisation, d'une culture: ici l'homme doit se fixer à lui-même des limites qui constituent le dessin d'une culture ... la "croissance zéro" n'est en rien la garantie d'apparition d'une culture nouvelle, seulement la possibilité ... C'est la fixation des limites qui est créatrice de liberté, contrairement à ce que l'on croit ... je ne crois que rien n'est aussi fondamental que ce problème des limites volontaires.*'
4. Castoriadis, *Labyrinthe*, V, p. 207: '*La seule limitation véritable que peut comporter la démocratie est l'auto-limitation, qui ne peut être, en dernière analyse, que la tâche et l'œuvre des individus (des citoyens) éduqués par et pour la démocratie ... Autant dire que la démocratie, comme la philosophie, écarte nécessairement le sacré ... elle exige que les êtres humains acceptent dans leur comportement réel ce qu'ils n'ont presque jamais voulu accepter vraiment ... à savoir qu'ils sont mortels.*'
5. Enzo Lesourt, *Survivre à l'Anthropocène*, Paris: Presses Universitaires de France/Humensis, 2018, pp. 63–120.
6. Cornelius Castoriadis, *Quelle démocratie? vol. 2* (*Ecrits politiques, 1945–1997, IV*), Paris: Editions du Sandre, 2013, p. 384.
7. Ibid., p. 387: '*L'autonomie, la liberté, n'est pas seulement l'abolition des contraintes externes ou des pulsions psychiques; elle est aussi l'établissement d'un autre type de rapport entre nos poussées profondes, individuelles ou collectives, et des instances capables d'en faire le tri, de leur donner forme ou de les empêcher de se manifester dans la réalité. C'est le rôle de la subjectivité réfléchissante et délibérante au plan individuel, des institutions démocratiques au plan collectif car la démocratie est le régime de la réflexivité collective et de la liberté autolimitée.*'
8. Jacques Ellul, *Sans feu ni lieu, Signification biblique de la Grande Ville*, Paris: La Table Ronde, 2003. Written in 1951, the text was first published by Gallimard in 1975.
9. Jean François Billeter, *Etudes sur Tchouang-tseu*, Paris: Editions Allia, 2004, p. 48.
10. Ibid., p. 48: '*plus qu'un rejet, il y a chez Tchouang-tseu* [Zhuangzi] *une critique radicale du pouvoir*'.
11. Ibid., '*[Guo Xiang] a transformé une critique acérée du pouvoir en une apologie de la démission et de l'indifférence morale. C'est en émasculant Tchouang-tseu* [Zhuangzi] *qu'il lui a assuré une place durable dans la culture des classes dominantes*'.

12. Ibid., p. 60: '*les hommes usent leurs forces et courent à leur perte parce qu'ils sont les jouets de leur propre vouloir*'.
13. Ibid., p. 61: '*la conscience peut … acquérir le pouvoir … de vouloir ou de ne pas vouloir, et se libérer par là de l'erreur.*'
14. Jacques Ellul, *Exégèse des nouveaux lieux communs*, Paris: Calmann-Lévy, 1966, p. 17: '*tous les hommes sont engagés dans un processus d'évolution commun … Notre monde est devenu total dans ses œuvres et ses expressions et cette unité dépasse de loin toutes les scissions fussent-elles aussi graves que la classe ou la nation.*'

BIBLIOGRAPHY

Adams, Suzi (ed.), *Ricoeur and Castoriadis in Discussion: On Human Creation, Historical Novelty, and the Social Imaginary*, London: Rowman & Littlefield, 2017.

Alleton, Viviane, *L'Écriture chinoise: Le défi de la modernité*, Paris: Éditions Albin Michel, 2008.

Andrews, Bridie, *The Making of Modern Chinese Medicine, 1850–1960*, Vancouver: UBC Press, 2014.

Appadurai, Arjun, *Modernity at Large: Cultural Dimensions of Globalization*, Minneapolis, MN: University of Minnesota Press, 2000.

——— (ed.), 'The Millennial Quartet 2: Globalization', *Public Culture* 12:1 (2000), special issue.

Ba Jin 巴金, *Miewang* 滅亡, Shanghai: Kaiming shudian 開明書店, 1929.

Baxter, William H. and Laurent Sagart, *Old Chinese: A New Reconstruction*, Oxford/New York, NY: Oxford University Press, 2014.

Beaud, Sylvie, 'La fabrique d'un patrimoine chinois: d'une production culturelle nationale à une tradition théâtrale locale' [The Making of a Chinese Heritage: From a National Cultural Production to a Local Theatrical Tradition], *Ebisu: Etudes japonaises* 52 (2015), pp. 291–321.

Wolfgang Behr, 'Role of Language in Early Chinese Constructions of Ethnic Identity', *Journal of Chinese Philosophy* 37:4 (December 2010), pp. 567–87.

Billeter, Jean François, *Etudes sur Tchouang-tseu* [Zhuangzi], Paris: Éditions Allia, 2004.

Boerdahl, Vibeke, *The Eternal Storyteller: Oral Literature in Modern China* (NIAS Studies in Asia Topics series, 24), London: Routledge, 1998.

BIBLIOGRAPHY

Børdahl, Vibeke, Fei Li and Huang Ying, *Four Masters of Chinese Storytelling: Full-length Repertoires of Yangzhou Storytelling on Video:Yangzhou pinghua sijia yiren: Quanshu biaoyan luxiang mulu* 揚州評話四家藝人: 全書表演錄像目錄 [Bilingual edition], Copenhagen: NIAS Press, 2004.

Bourdieu, Pierre, *Sur l'État. Cours au Collège de France (1989–1992)*, Paris: Seuil, 2012.

Bowles, Paul and Xiao-yuan Dong, 'Current Successes and Future Challenges in China's Economic Reforms', *New Left Review* 208:1 (1994), pp. 50–76.

Breckenridge, Carol A., Sheldon Pollock, Homi K. Bhabha and Dipesh Chakrabarty, 'The Millennial Quartet 4: Cosmopolitanism', *Public Culture*, 12:3 (2000), special issue.

Brook, Timothy, *The Confusions of Pleasure: Commerce and Culture in Ming China*, Berkeley, CA: University of California Press, 1998.

Castoriadis, Cornelius, *Fait et à faire. Les Carrefours du labyrinthe, vol. V*, Paris: Seuil, 1997.

———, *Histoire et création. Textes philosophiques inédits (1945–1967)*, Paris: Seuil, 2009.

———, *Quelle démocratie? vol. 2* (*Ecrits politiques, 1945–1997, IV*), Paris: Éditions du Sandre, 2013.

Chang, Eileen, *Love in a Fallen City*, London: Penguin Books Ltd., 2007.

Charbonneau, Bernard and Jacques Ellul, *Nous sommes des révolutionnaires malgré nous*, Paris: Seuil, 2014.

Chen Bian 陈晋 (ed.), *Mao Zedong dushu biji jiexi* 毛泽东读书笔记解析 [Mao Zedong's reading notes and analyses], Guangzhou: Guangdong Renmin chubanshe 广东人民出版社, 1996.

Chow Tse-tung, *The May Fourth Movement: Intellectual Revolution in Modern China*, Cambridge, MA: Harvard University Press, 1960.

Clover, Charles, 'China accused of waging war on Christmas', *Financial Times*, 26 December 2017, https://www.ft.com/content/d2236004-ea18-11e7-bd17–521324c81e23 (last accessed 2 January 2018).

Comaroff, Jean and John L. Comaroff (eds), 'The Millennial Quartet

3: Millennial Capitalism and the Culture of Neoliberalism', *Public Culture* 12:2, (2000), special issue.

Curtis, David (ed. and trans.), *The Castoriadis Reader*, Oxford: Blackwell, 1997.

Debord, Guy, *Society of the Spectacle*, Detroit, MI: Black & Red, 1983.

———, *Commentaires sur la Société du spectacle*, Paris: Éditions Gérard Lebovici, 1988.

———, *La Société du spectacle*, Paris: Gallimard, 1992.

———, *Correspondance*, vol. II, Paris: Fayard, 2001.

———, *Correspondance*, vol. III, Paris: Fayard, 2003.

———, *Œuvres*, Paris: Gallimard, 2006.

Demiéville, Paul, *Anthologie de la poésie chinoise classique*, Paris: Gallimard, 1962.

Deng Xiaoping, *Fundamental Issues in Present-Day China*, Beijing: Foreign Languages Press, 1989.

Dewey, John, 'New Culture in China', *Asia* 21:7 (July 1921).

Ding Ling 丁玲, *Shui* 水 [Flood *or* Water], Shanghai: Xin Zhongguo shuju 新中國書局, 1933.

Ding Zuxiang 丁祖響, and Burton Raffel 拉菲尔, *Zhongguo shige jinghua: Cong Shijingdao dangdai* 中國詩歌精华：从诗经到当代—*Gems of Chinese Poetry: From the Book of Songs to the Present* (Bilingual edition), Shenyang: Liaoning University Press 辽宁大学出版, 1986.

Dirlik, Arif, *Anarchism in the Chinese Revolution*, Berkeley, CA: University of California Press, 1991.

Duo Duo, *The Boy Who Catches Wasps* (trans. Gregory B. Lee), Brookline, MA: Zephyr Press, 2002.

Elliott, Mark C., 'The Limits of Tartary: Manchuria in Imperial and National Geographies', *The Journal of Asian Studies* 59:3 (2000), pp. 603–46.

Ellul, Jacques, *Exégèse des nouveaux lieux communs*, Paris: Calmann-Lévy, 1966.

———, *Sans feu ni lieu. Signification biblique de la Grande Ville*, Paris: La Table Ronde, 2003.

———, *Le Bluff technologique*, Paris: Fayard/Pluriel, 2012.

———, *Le Système technicien*, Paris: Éditions Le Cherche Midi, 2012.

Elman, Benjamin A. and Alexander Woodside (eds), *Education and Society in Late Imperial China, 1600–1900*, Berkeley, CA/London: University of California Press.

Fairbank, John K. and Merle Goldman, *China: A New History*, Cambridge, MA: Harvard University Press, 2006.

Fan, Shouyi, 'Highlights of Translation Studies in China Since the Mid-Nineteenth Century', *Meta*, 44:1 (March 1999), pp. 27–43.

Fogel, Joshua A. (ed.), *The Teleology of the Modern Nation-State*, Philadelphia, PA: University of Pennsylvania Press, 2005.

Füredi, Frank, *The New Ideology of Imperialism*, London/Boulder, CO: Pluto Press, 1994.

Furth, Charlotte, *A Flourishing Yin: Gender in China's Medical History, 960–1665*, Berkeley, CA/London: University of California Press, 1999.

Gaonkar, Dilip Parameshwar (ed.), 'The Millennial Quartet: 1, Alternative Modernities', *Public Culture*, 11:1 (1999), special issue.

Ge Jianxiong 葛剑雄, 'Zhongguo lidai renkou shuliang de yanbian ji zengjian de yuanyin' 中国历代人口数量的衍变及增减的原因 [Reasons for the rise and fall in China's historical population statistics], in *Dang de wenxian* 党的文献 [Literature of the Chinese Communist Party], No. 2, 2008.

Giles, Herbert A., *A History of Chinese Literature*, New York/London: D. Appleton and Company, 1901.

Gladney, Dru C., *Muslim Chinese: Ethnic Nationalism in the People's Republic*, Cambridge, MA: Council on East Asian Studies, Harvard University Press, 1990.

———, *Dislocating China: Reflections on Muslims, Minorities, and Other Subaltern Subjects*, London: Hurst & Company, 2004.

Guo Moruo 郭沫若, *Luoye* 落葉, Shanghai: Chuangzaoshe 創造社, 1926.

Harootunian, Harry, 'Quartering the Millennium', *Radical Philosophy: A Journal of Socialist and Feminist Philosophy* 166 (1999), pp. 21–9.

Hershatter, Gail, *Women in China's Long Twentieth Century*, Berkeley, CA: University of California Press, 2007.

Hobsbawm, E.J., *Nations and Nationalism Since 1780: Programme, Myth, Reality*, Cambridge/New York: Cambridge University Press, 1991.

Hsia, C. T., *A History of Modern Fiction*, 2nd edn, New Haven, CT/London: Yale University Press, 1971.

Hu Shi 胡適, *Hu Shi liuxue riji* 胡適留學日記, Taibei: Taiwan shangwu yinshuguan 臺灣商務印書館, 1959.

———, *Hu Shi wencun* 胡適文存, Taibei: Yuangong tushu gongsi 遠東圖書公司, 1953.

Hui Li, Ying Huang, Laura F. Mustavich et al., 'Y chromosomes of prehistoric people along the Yangtze River', *Human Genetics*, 122:3–4 (November 2007), pp 383–8.

Hung, Chang-tai, *Going to the People: Chinese Intellectuals and Folk Literature, 1918–1937*, Harvard, MA: Council on East Asian Studies, Harvard University Press, 1985.

Hunter, Holland, 'Tracking Economic Change with Ambiguous Tools: Soviet Planning, 1928–1991', *The Journal of Economic History*, 58:4 (1998).

Jiang, Lijing, 'The old, the new and the state in the making of modern East Asian medicine', *Studies in the History and Philosophy of Biological and Biomedical Sciences* 64 (2017), pp. 88–91.

Johnson, David, Andrew J. Nathan and Evelyn S. Rawski (eds), *Popular Culture in Late Imperial China*, Berkeley, CA: University of California Press, 1985.

Karlgren, Bernhard, *Grammata Serica: Script and Phonetics in Chinese and Sino-Japanese*, Stockholm: The Museum of Far Eastern Antiquities, 1940.

Kirby, William C., 'China's Prosperous Age: A Century in the Making', *China Heritage Quarterly* 26 (June 2011).

Kracauer, Siegfried, *The Mass Ornament: Weimar Essays* (ed. & trans. Thomas Y. Levin), Harvard, MA: Harvard University Press, 1995.

Lao She 老舍, *Lao Zhang de zhexue* 老張的哲學 [Lao Zhang's Philosophy], Shanghai: Shanghai yinshuguan 上海印書館, 1928.

Lee, Gregory B., *Troubadours, Trumpeters, Troubled Makers: Lyricism, Nationalism, and Hybridity in China and Its Others*, London/Durham, NC: C. Hurst & Co/Duke University Press, 1996.

———, *Chinas Unlimited: Making the Imaginaries of China and Chineseness*, London/Honolulu, HI: Routledge/Hawai'i University Press, 2003.

———, 'Le cadeau empoisonné de Versailles ou la Chine à la manivelle de l'orgue de barbarie', *Mouvements* 72:4 (2012).

———, *China's Lost Decade: Cultural Politics and Poetics 1978–1990—In place of History*, Brookline, MA/Lyon: Zephyr Press/Tigre de papier, 2012.

———, *The Eighth Chinese Merchant and the Disappeared Chinese Seamen*, iBook, 2015. https://itunes.apple.com/fr/book/the-eighth-chinese-merchant/id1044441047?mt=11

Lei, Sean Hsiang-Lin, *Neither Donkey nor Horse: Medicine in the Struggle over China's Modernity*, Chicago, IL: University of Chicago Press, 2014.

Lesourt, Enzo, *Survivre à l'Anthropocène*, Paris: Presses Universitaires de France, 2018.

Liang Qichao 梁啟超, 'Lishi yu renzhong zhi guanxi' 歷史與人種之關係 [The relation between race and history], *Yinbingshi wenji* 飲冰水文集, Taibei: Xinxing shudian 新興書店, 1955.

Louie, Kam (ed.), *The Cambridge Companion to Modern Chinese Culture*, Cambridge: Cambridge University Press, 2008.

Lu Hsun [Lu Xun], *A Brief History of Chinese Fiction* (trans. Yang Hsien-yi and Gladys Yang), Peking: Foreign Languages Press, 1976.

Lu, Tonglin (ed.), *Gender and Sexuality in Twentieth-Century Chinese Literature and Society*, Albany, NY: State University of New York Press, 1993.

Lu Xun 魯迅, *Lu Xun quanji* 魯迅全集 [Lu Xun's Complete Works], vol. 8, Hong Kong: Xianggang wenxue yanjiushe 香港文學研究社, 1973.

Marker, Chris, 'Interview with Cornelius Castoriadis, conducted by Chris Marker (English subtitles)', full version of an interview for Marker, Chris, *L'héritage de la chouette* ('The owl's legacy'), documentary broadcast in 16 episodes 12–28 June 1989 on La Sept, https://www.youtube.com/watch?v=5HL22xsVK4c (last accessed 7 February 2018).

Marx, Karl and Frederick Engels, with an Introduction by A. J. P. Taylor, *The Communist Manifesto*, Harmondsworth: Penguin Books, 1967.

Mignolo, Walter D., *Local Histories/Global Designs: Coloniality, Subaltern Knowledges, and Border Thinking*, Princeton, NJ: Princeton University Press, 2000.

Moncó, Beatriz, 'Entre la imagen y la realidad: los viajes a China de Miguel de Loarca y Adriano de las Cortes', *Revista Española del Pacífico*, 8:7 (1998), pp. 469–585.

Needham, Joseph and Wang Ling, *Science and Civilisation in China, vol. 1: Introductory Orientations*, London: The Syndics of the Cambridge University Press, 1954.

Ollé, Manel, *La invención de China. Percepciones y estrategias filipinas respecto a China durante el siglo XVI*, Wiesbaden: Harrassowitz, 2000.

Stephen Owen, 'What is World Poetry? Poets who write to be read in translation are a curious breed, as Bei Dao shows', *The New Republic*, 19 November 1990, pp. 28–32.

Paz, Octavio and Eliot Weinberger, *Nineteen Ways of Looking at Wang Wei*, New York, NY: New Directions, 2016.

Plaks, Andrew H. (ed.), *Chinese Narrative: Critical and Theoretical Essays*, Princeton, NJ: Princeton University Press, 1977.

Poirier, Nicolas, *Castoriadis: L'Imaginaire radical*, Paris: Presses universitaires françaises, 2004.

Rawski, Evelyn, *Education and Popular Literacy in Ch'ing China*, Ann Arbor, MI: University of Michigan Press, 1979.

Reischer, Rosalind, 'Protests threaten China's nuclear energy plans', *Global Risk Insight*, 26 August 2016, http://globalriskinsights.com/2016/08/nimbyism-threatens-china-nuclear-plans/ (last accessed 19 August 2017).

Ricoeur, Paul and Cornelius Castoriadis, *Dialogue sur l'histoire et l'imaginaire social* (ed. Johann Michel et al.), Paris: Éditions de l'EHESS, 2016.

Robertson, Roland, 'Comments on the "Global Triad" and "Glocalization"', in Inoue Nobutaka (ed.), *Globalization and Indigenous Cul-*

ture, Institute for Japanese Culture and Classics, Kokugakuin University, 1997, http://www2.kokugakuin.ac.jp/ijcc/wp/global/15robertson.html

Robinson, G.W. (trans.), *Poems of Wang Wei*, Harmondsworth: Penguin, 1973.

Rodes, Jean, *À travers la Chine actuelle*, Paris: Fasquelle, 1932.

Semanov, V.I., *Lu Hsün and His Predecessors* (ed. & trans. Charles J. Alber), White Plains, NY: M. E. Sharpe, 1980.

Shin, Leo K., *The Making of the Chinese State: Ethnicity and Expansion on the Ming Borderlands*, New York, NY: Cambridge University Press, 2006.

Skinner, G. William (ed.), *The City in Late Imperial China*, Stanford, CA: Stanford University Press, 1977.

Smith, Arthur H., *Chinese Characteristics*, Shanghai/London: *North China Herald* office/ Kegan Paul, 1890/2.

Têng, Ssu-yü and John K. Fairbank, *China's Response to the West: A Documentary Survey 1839–1923*, Harvard, MA/New York: Harvard University Press/Atheneum, 1954/63.

Thiesse, Anne-Marie, *La Création des identités nationales. Europe XVIII*[e]*—XX*[e] *siècle*, Paris: Seuil, 2001.

Wade, Geoff, 'The Polity of Yelang and the Origin of the Name 'China'", *Sino-Platonic Papers* 188 (May 2009), pp. 1–26.

Wade, Sidney, '13 Ways of Looking at Wang Wei', *Subtropics*, 20/21 (2016), pp. 174–8.

Waley, Arthur, *Chinese Poems*, London: George Allen and Unwin, 1946.

Wang, Zheng, *Women in the Chinese Enlightenment: Oral and Textual Histories*, Berkeley, CA: University of California Press, 1999.

Watson, Burton, *Chinese Lyricism: Shih Poetry from the Second to the Twelfth Century*, New York/London: Columbia University Press, 1971.

Wu, Jinglian, *China's Long March Toward a Market Economy*, San Francisco, CA: Long River Press, 2005.

Yang Gefei 楊格非 [John Griffith], *Xinyue quanshu* 新約全書 [The Complete New Testament], Hanzhen 漢鎮: 英漢書館 Yinghan shuguan, 1885.

Yang, Gladys (ed. & trans.), *Silent China: Selected Writings of Lu Xun*, London/Oxford/New York, NY: Oxford University Press, 1973.

Zhao, Jian, 'Japanese Loanwords in Modern Chinese', *Journal of Chinese Linguistics* 34:2 (June 2006), pp. 306–27.

Zhu Ziqing 朱自清 (ed.), *Tangshi sanbai shou* 唐詩三百首, Taibei: Dazhong shuju 大眾書局, 1976.

INDEX